REMOTE

WORK
IS THE WAY

IWO SZAPAR

REMOTE

WORK

IS THE WAY

A guide to making the most of our
office-optional future

This paperback edition first published in 2021 by

Iwo Szapar
www.iwoszapar.com

ISBN: 978-0-578-93561-4

This book arrived in the world at the best possible moment.

If Iwo didn't come up with the idea for this book, I'd have done it myself from the other end of the world. He has a great talent and an important mission.

If you thought remote work was about slacking off at home in sweatpants and slippers, you're wrong. It requires action, freedom, creativity. And most importantly, passion. And Iwo has it all!

This book will allow you to open up to the needs of employees and build a company that you would like to work for yourself.

Iwo has been at the heart of the remote worker community for years. Not only does he promote this style of life and work, but he is also a teacher for thousands of people who, thanks to his tools, have learned how to do it themselves from every corner of the world.

ANDREAS KLINGER
CTO of OnDeck, previously with Angel List, Product Hunt, Coinbase

Harmony between work and life is the basis of satisfaction. This book will help you find your own rhythm and balance.

PAUL ESTES
Leader in HR at Dell, Amazon, and Microsoft

Iwo teaches you how to adapt your work to your life, not the other way around. With this, you'll finally feel free.

JAROSŁAW KUŹNIAR
Journalist, businessman, and founder of Goforworld

INTRODUCTION

My manager doesn't trust that I'm doing my best when I'm not in the office. **What should I do?**

Keeping track of what my remote employees are doing is exhausting. How can I make it easier?

I love working from home, but **I feel isolated**. Is there a better way to stay connected to my colleagues?

Working outside of the office is growing in popularity and is more common now than it has ever been. Millions of people have discovered they **can do their jobs from home** ... or from halfway across the world. But while remote work comes with plenty of freedom and perks, it also comes with challenges. So how can you make the most of this new reality?

Co-founder of Remote-how, Iwo Szapar, has for years taught people how to **create remote-friendly work environments.** His guide to staying productive, avoiding burnout, and managing distributed teams is drawn from countless hours of collaboration with some of the top experts in the field.

Whether you work for yourself or a Fortune 500, this book is an invaluable resource for rethinking what the office-optional future means for you, your business, and the world. Inside is **a guide to the practical skills and habits** you'll need for communicating, collaborating, and getting the job done – as well as inspiration on how to live the kind of life you want. Remote work is the way of the future ... now it's time to find out how to make it work for you.

TABLE OF CONTENTS

PART ONE:

THE WORLD
OF REMOTE WORK

● ○

MORNING COFFEE: HỘI AN

I usually get up at 5 a.m. to watch as the world comes to life – regardless of whether I'm in the Vietnamese countryside, the bustling metropolis of New York or my hometown of Gdańsk, Poland. For over three years, my everyday life has included three intertwined parts: traveling around Asia, remotely managing a company in the United States, and keeping up with friends and family back in Poland. The scenery around me is constantly changing, but coffee at dawn is my ritual, no matter where I am. Sometimes it's a latte or americano, other times it might be a strong, cold Vietnamese coffee loaded with sweet condensed milk. When my day begins in an unusual place – say, a mountain hut somewhere in Indochina – I'll even settle for an instant Nescafe packet.

Today I drink a strong, black *ca phe den* here in the coastal town of Hoi An, Vietnam, as an endless hum of motorbikes and the buzz of nearby noodle shops permeates the morning heat. It is the end of March; a month from now, it will easily be over 95 degrees, even this early in the day. I am sitting at my favorite spot in town, 145 Espresso Cafe, as I check in with what the rest of the world has been up to while I've been asleep. I've got 68 new e-mails from my American and European colleagues and clients. Most of them have started working from home, as companies everywhere abandon their offices amid the COVID-19 pandemic. This trend means a major opportunity for Remote-how, the company I co-founded in 2017 that teaches organizations how to build and manage remote teams. Our services are in higher demand than ever before.

Half a year later, we are on the verge of bankruptcy. And I am at my limit.

INTRODUCTION

The idea for this book came to me in 2019. Remote work was then a niche phenomenon, and at the same time a dream of millions of people. We had been developing Remote-how for over a year and I felt more and more that I needed to explain not only how to work remotely, but also how this change would impact the whole world, far beyond the professional sphere. I passionately believed we had to ditch many of the old, prevailing ideas about how workplaces should function and rearrange the way we live our lives.

Then, in early 2020, COVID-19 happened. Overnight, the entire world faced a unique opportunity to free work from the physical constraints of offices. And it became clear that I could no longer wait. Now was the moment for this book. It was time to start writing.

The very creation of this book was a virtual effort. I wrote it from Vietnam, collaborating with people living in the United States and Europe, with whom I connected online more than once at every odd time of the day. I invited the best experts in the world, who have been blazing a path for remote work for many years, to join these pages. These are managers at some of Silicon Valley's most innovative companies – GitLab, Prezi, Mural, and others, and leaders at pioneering remote-first companies who agreed to share their knowledge with me and with you. However, the basis of what you're about to read is the knowledge and experience we've built over the years through Remote-how. Most notably drawn from our Remote-how Academy – the world's first remote work educational program for distributed team, which has so far supported over 400 companies. As well as our Remote Future Summit, the world's largest virtual conference devoted to the virtual work environment. Over the course of three years, more than 11,500 people from 129 countries took part in it.

IS THIS BOOK FOR YOU?
DEFINITELY, IF YOU WANT TO:

1. Decide for yourself when and how you work, to better balance your private and professional life.
2. Freely choose and change your place of residence to combine work with travel.
3. Work more productively, no matter where you are.
4. Peek behind the scenes to find out what life looks like for the most experienced remote workers and teams.
5. Understand how remote work will upend social norms and the lifestyle of the future.

Disclaimer: None of the people or businesses mentioned in this book received compensation for their participation, and these pages do not include any sponsored content. The knowledge and opinions expressed here are done so freely.

CHAPTER 1:

THE REMOTE REVOLUTION

POSITIVE CHANGE

Remote work may become the most powerful catalyst for positive change in the 21st century. Advances in technology are allowing us to redefine how we work and how we live our private lives. Being stuck in the office from 9 to 5 is no longer the standard. The work-from-anywhere lifestyle, once a luxury available to only a select few, is becoming a global phenomenon.

Working remotely is turning the world upside down.

- For some, it's the end ...
  - Of wasting 30 hours a month[1] on the daily commute to the office
  - Of being locked into life in a massive city (because "that's where the jobs are.")
- For others it's the beginning ...
  - Of redefining what is most important in life (Work? Family? Hobbies?)
  - Of having the freedom to choose where we live and where we travel
  - Of a world where everyone gets their own corner office

But there is a problem: our remote-friendly future isn't guaranteed. What if we don't take this unique, historic opportunity to radically change the way we work? It's possible that, after the pandemic fades away, we'll reluctantly slip back into the routine of office life. We might miss our chance.

The motivations for that change, however, are huge. Even pre-
-pandemic, people were eager for a new and more flexible way
of working. A survey conducted by Zapier in November 2019
shows that:

As many as **74%** of employees were ready to leave their current company in favor of one that would offer them the opportunity to work remotely.[2]

Before the pandemic, remote work was appealing to many types of people, including:

- Parents who wanted to reconcile work with childcare.
- Millennials keen to combine work with travel.
- People interested in working with foreign companies but not
  interested in relocating to a foreign country.
- Skilled workers in developing countries looking for a way to improve
  their lives through access to equally skilled work.

But it has been during the pandemic that remote work's appeal
has flooded beyond these niches and into the mainstream. In 2020,
many people had their first contact with working remotely – or,
more accurately, working outside the office. They're not exactly the
same. Remote work is, by definition, a job that can be done from
anywhere in the world; working outside the office, as many are doing now, is a forced, temporary solution during a crisis.

But even under these imperfect circumstances, people are
seeing the appeal of leaving the office behind. According to the

2020 surveys by Gallup and Adecco, more than half of the employees in the USA would like to obtain permanent remote work once the pandemic is over.

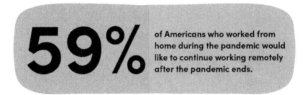

59% of Americans who worked from home during the pandemic would like to continue working remotely after the pandemic ends.

Still, it's not for everyone. The same research[3] shows interest in remote work varies depending on age, nationality, and family situation. For some, the office is just a better option. Though I've built a career evangelizing for remote work, I won't criticize such attitudes – my goal and Remote-how's mission has always been to enable everyone to have a *choice* in how they want to work (even if that choice is a more traditional office setting.)

> More than half of the employees would like to keep the workplace more flexible on a permanent basis. They should be given such an opportunity.

Our so-called "new normal" after 2020 opens companies to a reality in which, for many jobs, the physical location of work ceases to be important. Many are starting to understand the appeal! But adjusting to remote work in the long term is more complicated than the emergency measures taken during the pandemic. It's impossible to just copy-and-paste all of our in-office practices into a virtual environment; instead, organizations are going to have to fundamentally reconsider how they're managed and how they operate. It will be a painful process, one that requires us to overcome some of the age-old pitfalls of office culture. Pitfalls that include the lack of trust between employers and employees that leads bosses to micromanage their teams and workers to find ways to run out the clock each afternoon. For remote work to succeed as the "new normal," we have to ditch old habits and create new ones. If we don't, working remotely will end up a failed experiment.

THE BEGINNING OF MY REMOTE ADVENTURE

Imagine this: You dream, for years, of living a life that most people would consider impossible, until finally you seize the chance to make it happen. You start to turn that dream – of freedom, travel, financial independence, work-life balance, and global change – into a reality. You organize an international community of like-minded people and launch a company whose mission is to promote remote work, all while moving through 14 countries on three continents and turning your and your family's lives upside down. All this so that more people can choose how they will work and where to live.

Suddenly, overnight, the world turns upside down due to a pandemic. Millions of people find out for themselves that the place where they work does not matter. And that the world of offices in crowded cities will soon be obsolete. Even I, an unabashed optimist, never imagined this worldwide questioning of the status quo and embrace of my remote work utopian vision would happen so dramatically.

How did I end up on the vanguard of a remote revolution? I still pass for a teenager – the cashiers who regularly card me are always shocked to find I'm in my 30s – and have the heart of a high school partygoer. But I also deeply value my independence and like to decide about my own life without relying on others. I'm also not afraid to take matters into my own hands or take on challenges – even when others think my ideas are crazy.

It's been a year since my wife Ola and I landed in the charming Vietnamese town of Hội An. We planned to spend only a few months there, but fate had other ideas. Life moves slower here: whether

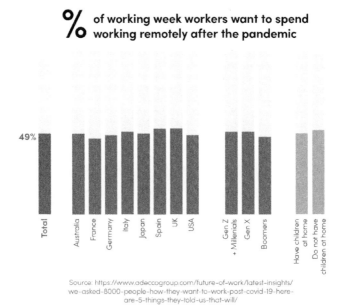

% of working week workers want to spend working remotely after the pandemic

Source: https://www.adeccogroup.com/future-of-work/latest-insights/
we-asked-8000-people-how-they-want-to-work-post-covid-19-here-
are-5-things-they-told-us-that-will/

it's a morning stroll on the beach, a scooter ride through green rice fields, or a coffee with a view of quaint Old Town. It is idyllic, but not only because of the landscapes. Hội An's locals are loaded with positive energy and smiles, even when we foreigners can only interact with them via Google Translate apps and sign language. When we left Poland four and a half years ago, I did not think there would be so many twists and turns in our lives that would change my view of reality.

I often think back to the hot summer of 2017, when we moved to Austin, Texas. Although I am always smiling myself – friends often tease me about my perpetually "sunny" demeanor – I have never been in a place so full of positive vibes before. With our new home came a new aura of freedom. We'd come to Texas thanks to my employer at the time, the German mobile shopping startup Shopgate. I'd visited the United States on a few business trips the previous year and experimented with a three-month stay in Phoenix, where I was smitten with the sun, heat, and swimming pool in every home. But the desert city didn't have "that something" I was looking for; instead, I fell in love with the idea of setting up shop in Austin, for a taste of something new.

I'll never forget getting home to Poland after one of my visits to Texas. Exhausted from jet lag, I was relaxing on the couch with Ola when I casually mused: "You know what? I'm just thinking...".

I didn't even have to finish my thought, Ola did it for me: "You want to move to Austin, right?"

I was shocked because we never talked about it. But maybe I shouldn't be surprised – after seven years together, Ola sometimes seemed to know me better than I did myself.

"Let's move to America!" is easy to say, but harder to do. First, I had to convince Shopgate that I, a 26-year-old Polish guy, could use my time in the U.S. to help them gain status as a global leader in the mobile shopping industry. I'd been working for the company for almost four years, but this would be a huge jump in role and responsibilities. It wasn't just my bosses that needed convincing – I also had to persuade American immigration officials that I was the necessary person for this job. It was the end of 2016; Donald Trump would soon assume the presidency and dramatically tighten immigration laws, making it even more difficult to import skilled workers from abroad.

And what about Ola? As my fiancée, she was not allowed to enter the USA on my work visa. There was only one solution: hold the wedding, ASAP! We organized everything in just two weeks – amazingly, it turned out better than I could have imagined. There's no need to stress over napkin colors and perfect invitation designs when you're in a hurry.

When we came to Austin, it wasn't terribly well-known abroad, and the Americans themselves had only recently caught on to its magic. Texas may have a reputation for cowboys, rodeos, desert landscapes, and conservative politics, but its capital is its cultural counterpoint. Austin is a city of green spaces, 10 months of summer, an international culinary scene with a fleet of food trucks (you won't find a better breakfast taco anywhere!), a center for live music, performance art, wild parties and cutting edge festivals (including the world-famous SXSW). In short: it is a city of freedom and a mecca for people who think outside the box. It stays true to its motto: "Keep Austin Weird."

In this amazing place, I had a major task – make Shopgate the leader in mobile shopping technology in the US. It did not seem unrealistic: we were already a leader in Europe and had been operating overseas for three years, with clients including then-NBA champions the Golden State Warriors. So we set ambitious goals: triple the number of employees in the USA to more than 100 people.

WHY REMOTE WORK?

Moving to Austin meant more than just moving to another continent. Our everyday routines changed, the way we looked at life and other people changed. In Poland, our environment was fairly homogeneous and our circle of friends is mostly made up of people we've known since school days. But Austin was home to a diverse, open-minded community made up of Texas natives, transplants from across the United States, and a vibrant crowd of international types. We had the chance to meet and befriend people from a wide range of backgrounds, skin colors, sexual orientations and religions. Austin welcomed them all with open arms, and so did we.

The change of environment made us rethink and reevaluate our priorities: what do we believe, what do we want, what are we striving for? Is the raise more important, or more free time? A trip to an exotic island, a DJ course or a new car? Or maybe on-the-job yoga sessions are better than that quarterly performance bonus?

We live in times when money ceases to be the main motivation for a growing group of people from wealthy countries. As the current economic and cultural climate drives more and more people to question the status quo, we are witnessing a redefinition of what is important in life.

> A vision of the company was born, a new venture that would help people get out of the office and out of the restrictive 9-to-5 cycle.

I started to think about it while hiring for the team at Shopgate. It was a candidate's market, and over and over, I heard from my American peers that their life priorities were completely different than those I was used to encountering in Poland. Trend reports bear this out: Surveys show that 77% of Millennials believe that flexible working hours make them more productive[4], almost 3/4 of them prefer to spend money on activities that will enrich them, rather than material goods[5], and a majority of workers would choose additional employee benefits over a straight salary increase.[6] And now, Gen Z is taking root in the labor market, building on the preferences of their Millennial elders and bringing an even more critical eye to our consumer society. On the way to becoming the best educated generation in history and even more critical of the world of material goods. In a December 2020 Wunderman Thompson Intelligence survey, 70% of Gen Z respondents said they would prefer to do work that they considered meaningful, rather than work that only paid a high salary.[7]

70% of Gen Z workers would rather do something meaningful than make a lot of money.

In Austin, I saw all this, not in charts and graphs, but with my own eyes. Younger workers are fueling a revolutionary shift by rethinking what should be at the center of our lives. It's a sentiment I share! Of course, despite the youthful momentum, this process is in its infancy and mainly happening in highly developed countries among people whose basic needs are already met. It is driven by the ranks of people who want to break out of traditional patterns. The growing need for freedom of choice and control over what our lives look like is and will be a priority in the coming decades. And though today's young people are often unfairly stereotyped as lazy or indifferent to the world beyond their digital screens, I have a completely different impression. I'd argue they're more motivated than any past generation to reshape the world, correct long-standing problems like inequality and climate change, and create an entirely new society.

There is a world on the horizon in which the end goal of work is something more than zeroes on a paycheck. Habits that developed as past generations sought other goals – bigger houses, fancier cars – will start to change. This philosophy of experience over possession will change the way we live and work. And right now it's strongest in those who've embraced remote work, who have already started to question the idea that "at work" and "in the office" have to be synonymous. I myself began to wonder: does this really make sense?

REMOTE WORK – A MODEL THAT MAKES SENSE

A brief history of work

THE HUNTER-GATHER AGE	THE AGRICULTURAL AGE	THE INDUSTRIALIZATION AGE	THE INFORMATION AGE	THE REMOTE-FIRST AGE
Humans are nomadic and roam the land for food and shelter.	The introduction of agriculture gives rise to location-dependent settlements.	Industrialization leads to mass migration to cities where jobs are available.	The emergence of Knowledge economy means even greater centralization of wealth in metropolitan hubs.	Technological innovation and globalization enables citizens across the world to acquire in-demand skills and work anywhere.

Source: https://blog.doist.com/remote-first-workplaces/

The eight-hour work day became popular in Europe and the United States a hundred years ago, after World War I. Since then, the world has gone through a period of the most intense technological and social changes in history. However, although our reality is radically different than it was a century ago, we're still stuck in work culture built around long outdated needs and ideas.

So why haven't our ideas about where and when to work evolved? Why are the routines of the early 20th century still shaping our lives? Isn't it time for a change?

Abandoning the 9-to-5 world with its sterile cubicles and soul--crushing commutes has long been a fantasy. Freelancers and tech entrepreneurs have paved the way, but until recently it was a lifestyle out of reach to most full-time employees. Slowly but surely, however, some companies started to rethink the obsession with the office. As more and more started innovating with work-from-home mentalities, the remote revolution started to gain traction.

Starting Remote-how was about convincing more businesses to overcome their skepticism and fears about remote work and helping them make the transition as smoothly as possible. No revolution comes without some mistakes along the way, of course, but my view has always been that it's better to act than to wait and wonder. At Remote-how, we have been supporting companies in building and managing distributed workforces for three years. It was a niche until the outbreak of the pandemic, but 2020 gave us a chance to go out into the open.

I consider it crucial not to waste this opportunity. Now is the moment for remote work to be implemented on a mass scale. We won't regret it – I know, because we've done the research. According to a 2018 survey by Remote-how and Kantar TNS, 95% of respondents who had the opportunity to work remotely assessed the experience positively or very positively.

95% of respondents who had the opportunity to work remotely said the experience was positive or very positive.

An overwhelming number! The report also showed that employees who work remotely are more likely to be satisfied with their work (94%) than those who do not (74%). And Buffer's State of Remote 2021 report found that 97% of remote workers would recommend this way of working to their friends.[8]

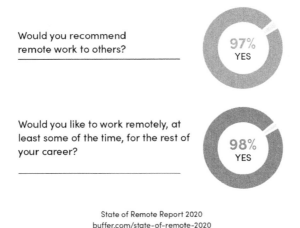

Would you recommend remote work to others?

97% YES

Would you like to work remotely, at least some of the time, for the rest of your career?

98% YES

State of Remote Report 2020
buffer.com/state-of-remote-2020

The data proves without a doubt that remote work is the way to go. From home, cafes, mountains, beach .... truly anywhere! Freedom of choice must be given to employees. Not everyone will decide remote work is right for them, but everyone should have access to it.

However, it is not enough to say: "Let's work remotely!" The need for systemic changes that will not happen overnight. It will be a long and arduous process, requiring perseverance from companies, employees and governments. But the payoff – for workers, for the planet, and for the future – is worth all of the effort!

CHAPTER 2:

IWO'S REMOTE REALITY

MORNING COFFEE: CHÀM ISLAND

It's May 2020, just after dawn, on this quiet island off Vietnam's central coast. I started my morning with an epic sunrise – my wife and friends were supposed to join, but I was the only one who woke up in time. I wasn't alone, though: the dog at our guesthouse saw me getting on my motorbike and hopped between my legs to join for the ride. My furry companion and I zipped across the island, from beach to breathtaking cliffs, to find a view more stunning than a Windows XP background. I realized we were nearly out of gas, but we made it back to the main harbor on fumes thanks to the magic of island scooters. Once there, my four-legged friend scampered off to play with the other dogs.

Now, in the sharp morning light, I'm settling into a low, red plastic stool with an icy black Vietnamese coffee, watching the island's morning market come to life. It's my first day off from work in weeks. We at Remote-how have been feeling intense pressure for months. Though the need for our expertise exploded amid the pandemic, so did pressure from our investors. The whole world is scrambling to figure out how to work remotely right now, and still we're struggling to convert our services into meaningful financial growth. It feels like we've been in crisis mode for too long. I feel helpless... I grab my phone, open my photos and think back to the first days of the company.

REMOTE-HOW: OUR ORIGIN STORY

From the very beginning, remote work was seen by most of its proponents as a way to shift life's center of gravity from work responsibilities to personal life. The idea was to adapt work to our daily lives – not the other way around. We needed to focus more on what was good for employees, not just what was good for companies.

As a Millenial in Austin's tech startup arena in 2017, I encountered enthusiasm for these ideas nearly every day from the people around me – and deep inside myself. I started to wonder if there was a way to take that idealism and turn it into a business.

I'd been bitten by the entrepreneur bug before, though none of my earlier start-up attempts had taken off in the way I'd hoped. This time, however, I could feel it was going to be different. I found myself disrupting local cafes at 7 a.m., confusing the American customers around me as I chattered away in loud, energetic Polish. I didn't care that I probably seemed a bit crazy to everyone around me – this was the only window of free time I had that lined up with European time zones.

I organized a series of virtual meetings: more than 40 interviews with HR experts and managers, finding out what they thought of remote work and its long-term viability. This is how I tested our first product ideas: all in a pale Texas dawn at beloved Radio Coffee in Austin.

The conclusions from the talks were optimistic. Remote work, according to nearly everyone I spoke to, had major potential. Every piece of data I encountered only fueled my belief that there was a need for an organization that could provide resources, education, support and expertise to those already working in fully or partially remote workplaces, or interested in giving it a try. I sensed the opportunity to build a company with a real and meaningful goal.

With that, Remote-how was born.

At stake? Changing the lifestyles of millions of people around the world and taking full-time remote work out of a tight niche and into the mainstream. Not just for freelancers and solo entrepreneurs, but for the everyday office workers who *also* deserved the chance to join a revolution and make their dreams come true. Already I could see the mission statement "We want to give everyone the freedom to choose when, where, and how they work."

Over time, the kernel of an idea would grow into a robust operation. Soon, I'd be joined by Marek Grygier and Magda Sowierszenko, friends from earlier in my career who shared my passion for meeting the needs of the remote-work future.

As Remote-how was starting out, only the tiniest fraction of employers were giving that remote future a chance. According to research conducted by Remotive, at the beginning of 2018, around 1,000 companies worldwide employed fully remote employees. Given that there are millions of businesses worldwide, that was a startlingly low figure. It meant a lot of work to do.

Part of that work would lie in convincing employers that giving more freedom to their staff was in their best interests. There was a fundamental mistrust that people would do their jobs if they weren't being watched – hence why working from the office, where the boss can peek over everyone's shoulder to make sure they're on task, was a must. (That employees could have Netflix running in another tab even while in the office didn't seem apparent to most of them, but I digress.) When that mistrust is baked into the company culture, it spreads to employees, too. Unfortunately, in most companies, fear of novelty often wins over responding to employee needs.

So how to convince employers that the work could still get done, no matter where the team was located? This question fueled Remote-how's very first products. We dreamed up the idea of a "workation," a combination of work and vacation that would allow companies to send employees on remote work trips to typical holiday destinations. The participants do their work together in an office, as they would back home, only this office is in an entirely different corner of the world. Remote-how would deal with all of the logistics of arranging the travel and the workspace, and also provide a series of training courses related to remote best practices, as well as leisure activities like surfing and wine tasting to add to the adventure.

Teams from PricewaterhouseCoopers (PwC), Ceneo and Netguru joined our first ever workation experiment in Lisbon, Portugal. The pressure was high, given that Remote-how's whole future depended on the success of this experience, and plenty of curveballs were thrown our way (including one of our residences alerting us that – surprise! – we'd have to move many of our participants out halfway through the trip.) It wasn't easy ... but it also ended up being a huge success! The PwC team even ended up winning accolades at the Employer Brand Management Awards 2019 for their work on the experiment.

But it gave us a lot to think about. Could we really scale a project like this in a meaningful way? Did we want Remote-how to be a remote travel agency in the first place? Plus, during all the months of work, we kept encountering the same mantra: "It sounds interesting, but we can't risk it, since our team doesn't have any experience in remote work yet." Fears of lost productivity were keeping companies on the sidelines. It started to become clear that what they really needed was earlier intervention. Could we find a way to better support businesses so that their employees learned the skills they needed to thrive in a virtual environment? We decide to focus on education.

By February 2018, an idea was born: bring together experienced remote workers to share practical knowledge via a dynamic virtual conference, the Remote Future Summit. My wife Ola got involved and soon we had a hardy team of 14 collaborators working to bring the conference from dream to reality. The first edition brought together more than 5,000 people from over 100 countries to participate in virtual workshops conducted by 64 speakers from top global brands, incl. Asana, Forbes or SAP. The outcome and positive reception exceeded our wildest expectations. We were earning international praise, and Remote-how was barely six months old. This was just the beginning.

From that very first conference, we found that people were starving for educational content — they wanted to learn how to do remote work better, but there was nothing on the market to help them figure it out. We would soon launch Remote-how Academy to provide structured resources, such as asynchronous video lessons and more, that would help fill this gap. Later, we'd experiment with a robust jobs marketplace geared toward finding full-time remote work, as well as virtual co-working, and grow into a global resource for remote professionals.

Today, we've become a platform with on-demand access to the world's best remote and hybrid work experts offering advisory services for companies at any stage. That access to hands-on consulting expertise and educational resources has helped more than 400 businesses and organizations to date.

REMOTE WORK: WHERE IT ALL BEGAN

Of course, the idea for remote work wasn't mine or Remote-how's alone. As far back as 1969, Allan Kiron, a scientist at the U.S. patent office, presented his ideas for combining computer technology with communication habits to create "dominetics" (aka domicile + connections + electronics) so that people could start doing more from the comfort of their homes.[9]

Four years later, a recession was spreading across the U.S. and the spike in oil prices hammered commuters; Jack Nilles, working for NASA, proposed telecommuting as an alternative to driving into the office every day. By 1979, IBM hit a major milestone: They made it possible for five employees to work remotely – full time! – for the first time. Within another four years, that number had jumped to 2,000; by 2009, as many as 40% of their 386,000 employees worldwide were able to perform their duties from home. The main factor determining this direction of development was the optimization of office maintenance costs. The company reduced their floor space by 7,000,000 square meters, saving nearly $100 million each year. Along the way, other companies, including American Express and General Electric, took notice and added their own remote options.

Still, remote work remained a niche. And for every step forward with a remote pioneer, there was a step backward with a remote skeptic. In February 2013, Yahoo! CEO Marissa Mayer announced the company would ban remote working. Employees who'd been granted the privilege of telecommuting didn't take kindly to having that benefit stripped away. It didn't go over well outside the company, either. Among those criticizing the decision was Virgin Group billionaire founder, Sir Richard Branson:

@richardbranson   Feb 25, 2013

Perplexed by Yahoo! stopping remote working. Give people the freedom of where to work and they will excel virg.in/fww

The ban on remote work was meant as part of a broader internal reform effort; according to Mayer, it was supposed to be a way to overcome the challenges of collaborating in a virtual environment. The most striking statement in her e-mail explaining it to the Yahoo! staff: "Many of the best decisions are made in the office, in informal meetings over coffee or in the hallway". Yes, her explanation was rooted in the eternal myth that only a physical space like an office can facilitate ties between employees and spontaneous exchange of ideas and inspiration around the water cooler. Later, however, it would come out that her real motivator for the change was data: She thought the numbers showed that those working from home weren't logged into the company servers enough.[10] Basically, the move ended up being a punishment for people not wasting time checking their e-mail more often.

> "If you aren't busy checking your email, I assume you're not productive."

That statement – absurd by today's standards – may have been one of the nails in the Yahoo! coffin. In 2014, the New York Times reported that more than 30% of employees left the company, and Mayer herself resigned in 2017. It goes to show: Nothing good comes from trying to stand in the way of a revolution.

REMOTE BUSINESS PIONEERS

Still, we have to wonder: Why has it taken half a century to popularize and normalize remote work? The major advancements we're seeing in the last two years are less about people finally being convinced and more about people and companies being forced by the pandemic to give it a try. COVID-19 accelerated the changes that had been going on for years but remained marginal. Matt Mullenweg, founder of WordPress.com, puts it best, saying that when it comes to remote work, "what's been holding us back is fear of the unknown, and attachment to the familiar.[11]

> **What's been holding us back is fear of the unknown, and attachment to the familiar.[13].**

But the way forward is inevitable. According to a Gallup study, in 2012, 39% of US employees worked remotely for a fraction of the time; by 2016, it was 43%. In 2019, remote work was recognized by LinkedIn as one of the four most important trends that will redefine the way we work.

LINKEDIN 2019:
TOP 4 WORKPLACE TRENDS

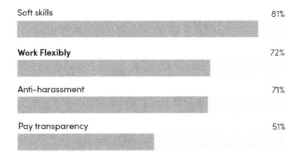

Soft skills	81%
Work Flexibly	72%
Anti-harassment	71%
Pay transparency	51%

What was the community of remote work-friendly companies like just before 2020? They shared a belief that if duties could be performed from anywhere, there was no point in forcing people to come to the office. They were committed to the idea that this wasn't just a business strategy, it was a way of making sure people got to be more human – spending more time with their families, on their personal hobbies, with the things that make them happy. In such organizations, the embrace of remote-work gave managers the opportunity to positively influence the lives of employees in a variety of ways. Many of those ways are neatly spelled out by the results of Buffer's State of Remote report:

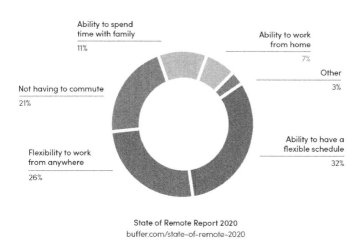

What's the biggest benefit you see to working remotely?

State of Remote Report 2020
buffer.com/state-of-remote-2020

Since the launch of Remote-how, we've aimed to be at the heart of the global family of #remotework advocates and the leading voices within it. We invited them to be speakers and participants in the first Remote Future Summit in 2018, which let us show them who we were and how committed we were to the concept, and that we could be useful allies. Interestingly, most of these relationships between #remotework leaders and Remote-how were built virtually right from the start, a major change from how I'd established professional relationships in the past. I felt how positively crazy these people were and saw that they really considered remote work as their mission.

Soon, after the summit, we were finally able to meet up in person, gathering outside of the virtual-only space for conferences – Running Remote in Bali and Nomad City the Canary Islands.

The Nomad City conference in Tenerife was a breakthrough. It was there that we tried co-living for the first time, thanks to which we got to know the remote pioneer community even better. For the less initiated: co-living is a place where you live, work and relax with other people. At the invitation of Nacho, the event organizer, we spent two weeks in one house with eight people we met only on the spot, all of them coming from Peru, the Netherlands, Spain, Switzerland, and the United States. They were employees of exciting companies who were already committed to remote culture, such as GitHub, Buffer, Mural or Remote Year. We had our own room, of course, but most of the time we stayed in common areas: places to work, cook or relax by the pool. It required us to go far beyond the comfort zone, but it quickly turned out that living in such a "communion" can be a fascinating experience. Although I was one of the conference speakers, I felt like an eager student. I gathered mountains of knowledge and inspiration from long conversations with people much more experienced in the field of working with dispersed teams. I got to see inside the world of an all-remote lifestyle with my own eyes.

These were the days when some of these pioneering companies had grown to considerable size. GitLab or Invision did not have an office, but they employed several hundred people and were valued at over a billion dollars each. Their founders openly admitted that remote work was the basis of success. More and more, outsiders were talking about their practices. When Automattic, the creator of WordPress and one of the pioneers of remote work, decided to take a break from their San Francisco office space in the summer of 2017, it sent shockwaves through Silicon Valley, which had so far been rather skeptical about the remote revolution.

CEO Matt Mullenweg decided to completely close down the office. The argument was simple – an average of only five people a day were utilizing the 15,000-square-foot space, even though it was available to the entire staff. That's not terribly surprising, since the company was also offering $250-a-month stipends to be used by employees who preferred co-working spaces or cafes close to home. Brilliant, isn't it?

Thanks to people like Matt Mullenweg, as well as Jason Fried and David Heinemeier Hansson (co-founders of Basecamp), Sid Sijbrandij (co-founder of GitLab), Amir Salihefendić (founder of Doist), Joel Gascoigne (co-founder of Buffer), and Wade Foster (co-founder of Zapier), remote work started to be seen as a hallmark of a successful, innovative business .... and also a benchmark for employee-friendly companies, perceived by many as ideal employers. Speaking a bit pompously: as your gateway to the world of freedom.

CHAPTER 3:

A DAY IN
THE REMOTE LIFE

MORNING COFFEE: HUẾ, VIETNAM

It's March 2020 and our vacation days in this small city are being interrupted by increasingly bad news. I've just learned that the borders of Vietnam have been closed. The government has realized the COVID-19 pandemic is no joke. For two months now, the country has been preparing for the worst. Given the lessons they learned from SARS in 2003, the Vietnamese know that the virus must be fought quickly and decisively. This morning ritual of indulging in caffeine from a scenic public cafe won't be an option for much longer: Full lockdown is coming, and no one knows how long it will last. Some fellow remote workers who'd been part of our community in Vietnam have already high-tailed it back to their home countries, but we're determined to ride this out. With that in mind, Ola and I make one of our best decisions of the year: We rent a beautiful, beach-side house with a few other friends. The world will stop, people will hide in their homes, and we will start living in a pandemic reality away from home – but at least we'll do it with a swimming pool and ocean views.

'REMOTE' DOESN'T MEAN 'AT HOME'

Many people got their first taste of *#remotelife* working from home during the pandemic. But in non-pandemic times, "remote" doesn't necessarily have to mean "in your own home." How was it before? Let's look at the data before the pandemic: where

did remote workers most often perform their tasks? It turns out ...
we're at home!

What location do you primarily work from?

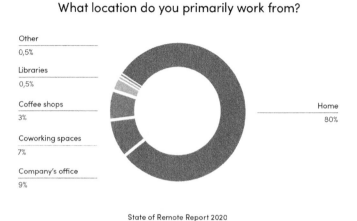

State of Remote Report 2020
buffer.com/state-of-remote-2020

As we consider what remote work will mean for us all in the future, we – both employers and employees – have to confront a number of not-so-easy questions:

- Do we want to work entirely outside the office, or do we want the option of going in for a visit sometimes?
- If we're outside the office, can we work from anywhere in the country?
- What about working in different time zones?
- What does it mean if everyone is in a different country? And if those countries change periodically?
- Are we *always* working remotely? Or only some of the time?

> Some dream of traveling unfettered. Others want the structure of occasional office time. One likes to work surrounded by a buzzing coffee shop, another prefers to work in solitude at home.

A study commissioned by Stanford University in May 2020 showed that in the post-pandemic reality, workers will have varying needs when it comes to remote work.

The point is, we all want different things. Just as "everyone has to be anchored to an office cubicle!" didn't meet everyone's needs or interests, neither will "everyone go work from your house!". Instead of one-size-fits-all approaches, we need a way to give people options – where ALL of the options are viable and productive. As we move forward, the most popular style of remote work may well be the one that gives people the most choices: a hybrid model.

In 2021+ (after COVID) how often would you like to have paid work days at home?

Never	20,3%
Rarely	19,1%
1 day per week	8,2%
2 days per week	11,1%
3 days per week	11,7%
4 days per week	5,4%
5 days per week	24,2%

Source: Response to the questions: "In 2021+ (after COVID) how often would you like to have paid work days at home?" Data from a survey of 2,500 US residents aged 20 to 64, earning more than $20,000 per year in 2019 carried out between May 21-25, by QuestionPro on behalf of Stanford University. Sample reweighted to match the Current Population Survey.

WHAT DOES HYBRID MEAN?

At its heart, the hybrid model means a workplace where expectations are that work can be done in a traditional office OR remotely from outside the office. For Company A, this might mean going hybrid on a local scale, where people stay in the same city or region, and just have the choice to not commute to an office some of the time; it saves time and commuting costs for employees, and potentially money for employers, who no longer need to provide desks and resources for a whole staff at once. For Company B, it might mean letting employees follow their paths – to that distant hometown, or a vacation destination, or long-term world travel – with just occasional, pre-scheduled visits to the company's HQ.

There are many ways to do this, and they are limited mainly by the company's guidelines and our imagination. Here, I present three variants that should be available to anyone who can work remotely.

- Option 1: office + home
- Option 2: office + home + external locations (cafes / co-working spaces / other)
- Option 3: home + external locations

Let us remember that there is no one perfect solution – everyone should check in which environment they work most efficiently and comfortably.

FULLY REMOTE AND BORDERLESS

As noted in Option 3 above, some companies might choose the extreme opposite of traditional office structures and completely abandon the idea of a physical workspace by making remote work the mandatory option. It's a structure that may appeal most to those seeking a travel-oriented lifestyle. We can choose from variants such as:

- **Workationist** – a person who takes off for a few weeks in a new spot, working their usual hours but spending their off time on holiday in a vacation-style destination. It's a chance to spend a longer break in, say, a beach paradise or mountain retreat than you'd be able to if you had to check out of work entirely and burn valuable vacation hours.

- **Slowmad** – a person who moves from one location to another for longer stretches, living a "normal" life (rather than a "vacationer" life) in each new spot. This is great for people trying to avoid harsh winters and chase the sun year-round, or who find inspiration from new surroundings. Many slowmads may retain a home base in their home countries, but much of their life is outside of that.

- **Digital Nomad** – a person who completely abandons the idea of maintaining a home base, lives minimally from a suitcase, and moves from place to place on a constant adventure. This variant may be the most famous type of remote worker (no thanks to the Instagram-driven stereotypes of 20-somethings building businesses from Bali swimming pools) but also the most rare, as personal circumstances and professional responsibilities rarely offer this kind of freedom for anyone other than self-employed freelancers and the occasional lucky full-time employee.

My heart is closest to the last two variants, which is why a typical working day that I describe in this chapter takes place in Asia.

HOLIDAY HAPPINESS

Thousands of years ago, we were all nomads; eventually, the demands of agriculture and civilization led us to start staying in one location – settlements and then cities – more permanently, for the sake of stability. Almost everything has changed in the world since then, but the attachment to the workplace continues to this day.

Currently, however, the number of people who want to change their surroundings is growing. Ola and I count ourselves among the group craving a life of travel. Recently, Facebook reminded me of my post from 2014. We were then on our first holiday together in Asia. During our trip around Thailand, we stopped at the fairy-tale island of Ko Yao Yai. "We're moving here!" Ola joked ... but for me, it's when the idea of a traveling worklife took serious hold.

It took awhile, but we got there eventually. We left Poland in 2017. After a year and a half in the USA, we set out to explore the world. We visited 14 countries, with longer stays in five, including over a year in Vietnam (as I write these words, we do not know yet how long we will stay here). Earlier, when we did not have such a smooth combination of work and life, vacations were a way to save our sanity. Each of us has places where we go with great pleasure, to enjoy the landscape or climate, play our favorite sport or just get to know the area. The environment (where and with whom we are) around us and the kind of stimuli our brains encounter can have a major impact on our well-being. Don't believe me? It's science! In fact, a study[12] published in the journal Nature Neuroscience in 2020 found that people who filled their days with new, unique, or exciting experiences (the way we often do when traveling, and don't when we're locked at home during a pandemic) are notably happier. Those exciting experiences trigger activity in the hippocampus and the striatum—aka the parts of our brains that make us feel rewarded.

I mean, who doesn't love a vacation, right? A time when we can do whatever we want. Some people like to… do nothing. Others pursue hobbies and passions. This is what the appeal of free time is all about – we decide ourselves what to do with it. The problem is that there is never enough time. Never! I have yet to meet anyone who would say he has enough days off. That is why I started to wonder: why do we work for over 90% of the year? Often from the uninspiring cage of the office? Even I, a self-conscious workaholic, have come to the conclusion that something is wrong.

The good news, of course, is that remote work can help with that problem. The benefits we draw from holidays away – renewed energy, new inspiration, and more – don't have to remain limited to occasional escapes when we're 100% work-free. Travel, change of environment, new activities – all these have a positive effect on how we feel. So what if each of us had more control over our lives and was free to choose an environment that gives us pleasure and relaxation? And to achieve this, he would not have to take a limited vacation? Bingo! That's where remote work comes into play.

I've been living in this reality for three years myself, and I can assure you that the freedom to choose gives me a huge dopamine kick every day. I am writing these words after a weekend spent traveling the winding roads of northern Vietnam. During the week we focused on work, but we still found time to admire the magical sunrises and sunsets in the Sa Pa valley or to go to the highest peak in Vietnam, Phăng Si Păng (Fansi-pan) to look at the world from a height of over 10,000 feet above sea level.

There have been many such places and moments in the last few years, all fueled by our passion for discovering the world while working.

A DAY IN THE LIFE OF IWO

I wanted to present to you a tidy, inside look at a "typical" day in my life. But while preparing to write this chapter, I realized how different my days often are. In recent years, I've spent days working everywhere from a desk in a Polish co-working space, to a sunny Portuguese beach, to a crowded Hong Kong cafe. My work also varied: some days I was organizing status meetings for a team scattered across time zones 10 hours apart, other days I was giving a live lecture to 600 Deloitte employees with swaying palm trees in the background, or participating in a strategy workshop from the roof of a Hanoi restaurant.

Despite all the variations and unpredictability, one thing was always my inseparable companion – the Internet. Well, maybe except for a week in Cambodia, when we had to creatively look for ways to contact the world due to the notorious power cuts. As a result, we moved many of our tasks offline, which resulted in intensive conceptual work, without meetings or e-mails.

Skeptics will see where we are and assume we're slacking off. "Oh, are you on the beach? Are you having a nice vacation?" We have learned to fight it in the best possible way, that is, by behaving 100% professionally. We work full time, and take our jobs seriously, even amid the wildest surroundings. In our world, it doesn't matter *where* we perform our tasks. The environment changes ... but the work always gets done.

ABOUT 5:30 A.M. – EARLY START

I know, I know: Many of you are seeing that I wake up at this inhumane hour and you're ready to throw this book away and give up on the idea of remote work. Don't worry! It's just my own, weird choice – not a requirement for a successful remote life. Everyone can adjust their schedules to their own preferences. I wasn't always such an early bird. But once I shifted from working for a company to creating my own with Remote-how, I found I needed a new rhythm to keep my days on track. It started as a short-term experiment, but I soon realized getting an early start was the best way for me to ensure a productive, satisfying day. I remain faithful to it to this day.

5.30-6.30 A.M. – COFFEE WITH A VIEW OF ...

My wife does not share my enthusiasm for early starts, so I try to sneak out of bed quietly. (It doesn't always work, so often our first exchange of the day is Ola cursing and me apologizing.)

The next step is my morning coffee. It tastes best when it comes with a good view, whether it's of the coursing Colorado River in Texas or of water buffaloes stretching lazily amid swaying Vietnamese rice fields. I try to enter each day calmly and avoid rushing or stressing.

I often start my day at a local coffee shop. In Asia, locals like to get up early, so I have no problem finding places open by 6 a.m. It is also the time to go shopping. Soon both the café lady and the saleswoman at the market are your friends, even if they know little or no English. This is great fun and extends the list of places and situations where you feel good. Your happy places.

Over coffee, I start scrolling through the messages and e-mails that arrived from my team and our clients and partners while I was sleeping. Really, I should give myself more of a break and save the work for later, but it's a bad habit and I can't help myself. I hope one fine day the Gmail app will disappear from my phone.

6:30-10 A.M. – VIRTUAL MEETINGS OR
ACTIVE MORNING?

The schedule for this part of the day depends on whether or not I have appointments with people in other time zones. If so, I greet myself with a dry joke about "greetings from the future" or I say that "I'm just drinking my first coffee, so I may still have a problem expressing myself". That's how it is: we are starting Tuesday in Asia, and someone is ending Monday on the west coast of the United States.

As much as I love my morning caffeine, I draw just as much energy from the conversations I have in the virtual office first thing in (my) morning. They always charge me with a dose of positive vibrations for the whole day. I love talking to people; I get great pleasure from it, even if it is a 100% virtual meeting with total strangers.

On days when I don't have meetings, I try to fit something active into my morning. In Bali, I got into yoga (I used to laugh at it, now I love it!). In Vietnam I tried stand-up paddleboarding on the ocean. In Poland, I'd go cycling or walking with my favorite music blasting in my ears. I usually don't care for the gym, but these days I've started making the effort to go regularly and I've learned to love it. (I should take this moment to confess: some days start not with virtuous physical activity and work ... but with lying on the couch flipping through YouTube and Instagram. Hey, nobody's perfect!)

When I get hungry, I look for local breakfast delicacies. In Vietnam, I usually choose the delicious *phở* soup or *bún thịt nướng* (rice noodles with meat and vegetables). Tasty, healthy and very cheap! Good food puts me in the right mindset for the day. So does good weather – the more sun and blue skies, the easier it is to get going. Dull, gray mornings just aren't as motivating ... that's why the freedom to choose where and when you wake up really helps!

10 A.M. – 2 P.M. – FULL FOCUS

Regardless of where I am and what my morning looks like, I spend this part of the day on deep work. This is the time when I keep my calendar free from meetings and avoid any distractions. I'll spend time responding to clients and partners, as well as collaborating with my team on ongoing projects and offering feedback. I can do a lot of this type of work asynchronously – meaning, without needing the other person to be awake or engaged at that time. Mid--afternoon Asia-time ends up being perfect, as it means colleagues in Europe and the U.S. will have messages from me right as they start their days.

I work in intervals – depending on the type of task it is, about 45-60 minutes of work and 5-10 minutes of break. The rhythm and structure help me a lot, as does the preparation of a suitable work environment (offline and online), precise determination of what I intend to achieve, and the freedom to combine duties with pleasure. I'll discuss this all in more detail in Chapter 7's guide to productivity; for now, though, here are a few factors that help me while working:

1 WORK ENVIRONMENT

I like changing locations, to shake things up. One thing must be true about each place: I must feel at ease. Complete comfort is the key to being as productive and efficient as possible. I regularly change places in a co-working office or cafe several times, until I find the one that's "just right." Sometimes I'll try a strategy (first recommended by my friends at Buffer) called "workstation popcorn" – meaning, I'll finish one specific set of tasks, then change locations before setting into the next set of tasks.

Moving helps break things up, and changing the environment can help, especially with creative work.

I also need to make sure I have the right gear. First: I must have a great set of headphones. They help me disconnect completely

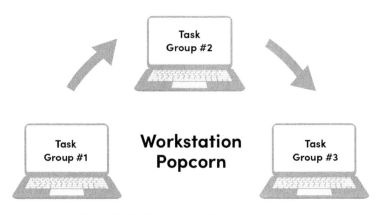

Source: https://buffer.com/resources/5-ways-to-get-more-doneby-working-smarter-not-harder/

from my surroundings, no matter what's going on around me. (For example, I'd never be able to concentrate on writing this chapter if my headphones weren't drowning out the sound of kids screaming and playing on the beach nearby.) With headphones I am transported to a different reality. I've been using the same pair for three years, and they've been a breakthrough for me in terms of efficiency in noisy places. Ola got a pair of her own, in part so she doesn't have to hear me shouting on calls or to myself.

Second: My traveling computer stand. Sometimes, yes, I just work with my laptop on a table or my lap, but since discovering the stand two years ago, it has made a world of difference in creating a more ergonomic set-up for long work sessions from cafés or co--working spaces.

#2 TASK ORGANIZATION

Three tools help me manage my work chaos every day:

- **Asana**, a task and project management tool, helps me plan my work according to the priorities of the projects I am involved in. We've been using it since the very beginning of Remote-how's existence, but there are lots of other options out there, depending on your needs and work style: from Todoist, ideal for personal task management, to platforms such as Trello, Basecamp or Wrike, designed for team work. The choices are plentiful.
- **Google Calendar** helps me keep track of my responsibilities – both professional and private – by connecting my two worlds. It keeps my daily work rituals and endless meetings in order, and also keeps track of personal activities like my gym sessions, dentist appointments, or social engagements with friends. This makes it easier not only for me to manage my time, but also for my team members to know when I am available.
- **Toggl Track** is an amazing time-tracking tool that shows how long I spend on certain activities or areas of work. It helps me stay on task and work as efficiently as possible.

These are the three main pieces of my puzzle, but there are plenty more – we'll get into that in Chapter 7.

3 TIME MANAGEMENT

I've tried several times to precisely track my working hours. These attempts usually ended in failure – after a few days or weeks, I'd just forget about it. The breakthrough came when I decided to see not just how much time I spend "at work," but how much time I actually spend working. If I read my first e-mail at 6:30 a.m. and my last meeting with a client is at 10:30 p.m., do I actually work 16 hours? Of course not! But because there is so much flexibility in my working hours, I couldn't tell how much of it I was actually being used for productive work. When I analyzed the data from more than six months of daily use of Toggl Track, I found I was online around 12 hours a day and spending about 8-10 hours completing tasks and working cleanly. To improve my efficiency, I turned to the Pomodoro method of working in intervals. Most people who suggest this method use 25-minute intervals focused on one task; I prefer to extend them to 45-50 minutes. My phone goes away, I limit myself to one browser window, and focus in on a single objective. After each interval, it is time for a 5-minute break to clear my head before starting the next thing.

2-6 P.M – BREAK TIME AND TEAMWORK

At some point in the afternoon, I make sure I take a break for 1-1.5 hours. This could mean going out for lunch with friends, or grabbing a bite on my own to relax. It gives me a moment to breathe and refresh before the second part of my day, which revolves around collaborative work with my Remote-how colleagues. Since I'm in Asia at the moment, my late afternoons and evenings line up with the heart of the European work day. This is when our status meetings are held, and when we gather for joint work on projects or just to catch up and bond. My colleagues and I like each other, we are on the same wavelength and we always have something to talk about. I love to talk, so often, before we move on to the business part, we often spend some time discussing world news, politics, new developments in our industry or what's going on in our personal lives. But when we move on to Remote-how topics, we shift into fully professional mode: Following the agenda, taking notes and staying on mission. Sometimes all this happens while I'm sitting at my desk; other times it's while I'm wandering a beach or city streets. No matter where or how – it's important that work is in full swing!

6-10 P.M. – MORE WORK OR ... TIME TO EXPLORE!

My evenings have two faces. Most often they are a continuation of the working day: more meetings, e-mails, projects. Sometimes, however, I can break free and set out to explore whatever area we're in that day. Ola and I are avowed foodies, so our journeys are often focused on culinary experiences. An ordinary Tuesday evening for us could rival the best food vlog episode, as we explore street food, night markets, and local restaurants for the tastiest options with just one rule: As local as possible! We don't save the fun for the weekends: Any day is a good day for an adventure. After that, it's a matter of winding down before a good night's rest. Ola and I made a rule for ourselves: No electronics at bedtime. Our addiction to non-stop scrolling on our phones was impeding our sleep, so we decided to give devices a rest and keep them out of the bedroom. I've even switched to a watch for alarms so that there's no excuse for my phone to be a distraction before bedtime.

FIRST-HAND

A DAY IN THE LIFE OF OTHER REMOTE WORKERS

My type of workday isn't the only one. Everyone who works remotely has a different type of job, different physical location, different set of personal circumstances, that can shape how they structure their time. Here, let's break away and see how five other people – a family-focused mom, a night owl, an adrenaline junkie, a small-town innovator, and an international backpacker – live their remote lives:

FAMILY FIRST

Katina, 48 years old
Digital Marketing Director

Why I went remote ...
My commute put me in the hospital for stress-related illness twice in six months. My mom died young, and health concerns aside, spending hours a day every day stuck in a car seemed like a waste of precious time.

Morning ...
I make coffee and feed my spoiled cat. Put on headphones with Brain.fm to get focused.

Afternoon ...
Take a break to either walk outdoors or catch up with my daughter. She's in high school, so I try to keep our relationship healthy before she heads off to college.

Evening ...
Catch up with my husband and enjoy dinner with my family.

What changed after going remote ...
I've been able to prioritize my health in general, and mental health especially. Plus I now have less mom guilt! I can better support my kids, and I also have time to nurture friendships.

NIGHT OWL

Mitasha, 32 years old

Human Resources Specialist

Why I went remote …

In 2018, my father had a health emergency and I had to move from the United States back to a small city in India to be his caregiver. Between my family's needs and the pandemic, going remote was not just personally beneficial, it was also the only socially conscious choice.

Morning …

Since I'm a night owl, my mornings are so much more relaxed now! I wake up to a cup of breakfast tea, a 15-minute mindfulness routine, water my plants and do a face mask.

Afternoon …

This is when I'm busiest with work and calls. I have a light, nutritious lunch. I've started skipping caffeine and recharging with short walks or family time to beat the snooze blues.

Evening …

I'm more anxious in the evenings than I was when I worked in an office, mostly because I feel guilty about productivity or deadlines. I try to disconnect for a few hours during dinner by turning off notifications and separating from my work laptop.

What changed after going remote ...

I have more time for personal pursuits: I joined a book club, published my writing and started investing! I'm also in a long distance marriage — working remotely is one of the best ways to balance my professional growth, caregiving responsibilities and a relationship. I appreciate that moving back to my hometown lets me improve my standard of living. At the same time, I do miss the energy and motivation that comes from being surrounded by likeminded people working toward a common goal.

ADVENTURE HUNTER

Greg, 31 years old

CEO and Marketing Entrepreneur

Why I went remote ...

Office life severely limited my creativity. The high intensity of my work requires me to reset my mind regularly; this can be done much more efficiently by surfing, climbing, or sailing than by moving through a concrete jungle.

Morning ...

I start the day early. I'll do interval training on the beach and swim, then do a yoga or meditation session. After that, I can afford a healthy breakfast (mainly local fruit, seeds, and fats). Finally, a shower. It takes a while, but it allows me to enter a demanding 12-14 hour working day with a clear head.

Afternoon ...

First, I do creative work. Then it's time for lunch and a siesta. I make time to explore nearby towns, walk on the beach, or have a strong coffee from the espresso machine. Then, I move on to more technical and "productive" tasks.

Evening ...

Evenings are the time of reward. When I get out of my duties, I get to know the local evening life wherever I'm staying. It is also a moment to catch inspiration by talking with people or calm down in solitude.

What changed after going remote ...

I have a greater understanding of the value of time. I've found work doesn't have to be a punishment. It can only be part of the way of life. It is also about learning efficiency, responsibility, and discipline. After all, it's a chance to inspire others to make positive changes in life and act in harmony with yourself.

RURAL INNOVATOR

Brett, 30 years old
Manager, "Future of Work" Program

Why I went remote ...

I'm not always productive for long hours in an office. I like the freedom of managing myself. If I'm tired, I'll take a nap and then get back to it. I also wanted to stay in Atlanta, but not limit my options to Atlanta employers.

Morning ...

I usually go to my co-working space for breakfast. It's great to feel like I have in-person "co-workers" even if we don't work together.

Afternoon ...

I have the flexibility to cook lunch or start preparing dinner early. It's allowed me to eat healthier and save money on food.

Evening ...

I have a part-time remote role as well, so I often work to earn extra money.

What changed after going remote ....

I'm much more productive, I've become more organized and I have more free time — and that has always been my goal.

REMOTE BACKPACKER

Chelsea, 27 years old
Web Designer and Brand Strategist

Why I went remote ...

I started as a backpacker and fell in love with the discovery life-style. I knew I needed to create an online income for myself so I could keep living the adventure life.

Morning ...

I wake up and put music on right away. I shower, tidy wherever I'm staying, and jump right into checking e-mails. Then I go to the gym or for a walk and plan out my schedule based on client needs or sightseeing activities I've planned to have that day.

Afternoon ...

It depends: Sometimes I'm working away, smashing out client projects; other times I'm roaming around the city, visiting a beach, going on a new adventure.

Evening ...

I try to finish work in the afternoon so that in the evening I can relax, roam around, go out for meals or drinks, watch the sunset or (after busy weeks) make a massive veggie meal and chill out at 'home' to a Netflix documentary.

What changed after going remote ...

I had to figure out the right work/adventure balance as my business started to grow very quickly. I had to hire the right team of assistants to help me.

CHAPTER 4:
THE REMOTE WORKER

MORNING COFFEE: AUSTIN, TEXAS

It's 6:30 a.m. in January 2018. I order an espresso to sip while taking in the view of the Colorado River from my favorite table at Mozart's Coffee Roasters. I'm at a major turning point: two days ago was my last day working for Shopgate and I'm about to embark on making Remote-how a reality. Starting a new company – even one I believe in fervently – means risking every penny Ola and I have saved over the years. And without my full-time Shopgate role, we'll have to leave behind not only our financial security, but also our beloved Austin – but to go where? Everything is uncertain right now ... yet somehow, I'm excited, even optimistic. At this moment, I can't foresee the ups and downs we'll encounter on this adventure – we'll be on the verge of financial collapse one month, then riding high on investor input by the end of the year. But I do know, even in these early days, that it will all be worth it.

MY REMOTE ORIGINS

My first taste of remote work came long before Remote-how. In 2011, I landed an internship at an interactive agency and was tasked with creating a lifestyle website from scratch. After several organizational meetings in the office, each of the trainees was allowed to choose the method and place of work. I chose a remote one: first from Warsaw cafes, and then from Berlin, where I moved to improve my German. For most of the summer, I combined the management of the portal with a job as a waiter's assistant, putting in 12 hours a day. Technology for remote work was just in its infancy, and we desperately needed better organization, but somehow we made it work. After that, feeling entrepreneurial, I embarked with a friend on plans for a social commerce platform – PonPon, a sort of variation on Pinterest – all while collaborating remotely. A year later, at a technology fair in Germany where I was searching for strategic partners, I got to know Shopgate, the shopping platform for online stores. In 2012, there wasn't much focus on mobile sales. I saw nothing but potential, and spent the next few weeks bombarding Shopgate's CEO with e-mails and presentations, trying to convince their top brass that Poland was the next market worth developing.

I got the green light, a small salary and a paid co-working office. It was my first time working in such a place and I was a little flustered, but the community of Noa Co-working, one of the first co-working spaces in Warsaw, welcomed me with open arms. I spent almost a year with them. Then we moved to our own office, where 25 people worked at its peak, and PayPal and Mastercard became our strategic partners.

Today, when I think about the key to the success of that venture, one of the most important words in remote work comes to my mind: trust. Andrea and Ortwin, the co-founders of Shopgate, took the risk. They hadn't worked with me before they brought me on board, but they had the good faith to know I'd do good work even if they weren't standing over me, watching me. From day one, our relationship was based on mutual trust. And also on my trust in myself. I was wondering: can I do it? Is this type of work right for me? I had to find the motivation within myself to avoid distractions and temptations, and get the job done.

CAN ANYONE BE A GOOD REMOTE EMPLOYEE?

Most of us dream about remote work. However, we rarely wonder why it is so – that is, what motivates us to work remotely – and what format would be optimal for us. Would we thrive most as full time employees working 100% remotely, or combining remote and office work? Would we be happiest combining more formal jobs with additional projects and freelancing gigs? Would we feel most energized if we were our own boss, managing a remote company or operating as a freelancer or consultant?

Motivation is a very individual matter, but what matters most is having the choice beyond a 9-to-5 in the first place. For me, my primary motivation was my fascination with the possibility of working from the farthest corners of the world. Since Ola and I started living this remote way, we've talked to many people who express longing for a lifestyle like ours. "If only my company would let me work remotely, I would also travel much more," they lament. I'm not surprised. Even I'm still easily taken in my photos of laptops and #nomadlife hashtags. It could be beaches, mountains, or anywhere else – that picture-perfect Instagram version of #remote-life is the stuff of fantasies.

The problem is, the world is rarely as perfect as all those posed photos – which never show the hardships of travel, or the screaming kids in the background, or the construction zone just outside the window. Remote work can be a challenge that not everyone can meet. We are different, so the freedom that remote work gives us, we must adapt to our lives and prepare to introduce changes. It will mean a different set of activities for everyone, often interfering with private life.

7 FEATURES OF THE IDEAL REMOTE EMPLOYEE

Remote work is not for everyone! Some people take to it like a fish in water; others need more time to adapt. What character traits and skills do you need to be happy working remotely? Maybe you already have many of them, but you don't know it yet. Here, I'll list some of the characteristics you need to succeed remotely – it's up to you to determine if they're skills you already possess, or if they're areas you need to work on before you break free of the office. The reward, if you have or learn these skills, is freedom, and the satisfaction that comes with it.

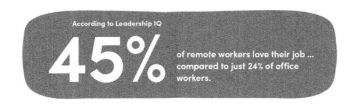

According to Leadership IQ

45% of remote workers love their job ... compared to just 24% of office workers.

When looking at the following list of characteristics that the "ideal remote worker" should have, you will notice that many of them coincide with the characteristics of the "ideal office worker". Companies should pay more attention to many of them, but often they only look at the so-called hard skills, instead of how their workers operate. The list is the result of dozens of conversations with recruitment specialists for remote work and managers running distributed teams. It includes both the character traits that are sought during the recruitment process and the skills facilitating effective remote work.

1 MOTIVATION AND AMBITION

Motivation is the key to success in a remote environment. Remote employees are very often people with great passion who can find the necessary inspiration themselves and consciously pursue their own aspirations. In the office, it is easier to draw energy from the people around us and motivate each other. In the case of remote work, this is not possible, which is why recruiters often look for people who implement their own projects or passions outside of work hours. It can be anything that is not related to work: crocheting, running a healthy eating blog, supporting an animal shelter, or even that money-making side hustle. The key is to have the energy and drive to move forward because you're passionate about it.

2 CONSCIENTIOUSNESS AND DISCIPLINE

Successful remote workers do not need to be encouraged or pushed to act all the time. They are responsible and disciplined. You will not have a "supervisor" checking that you are sitting and clicking. You have to watch on your own to perform your tasks.

3 SELF CONFIDENCE

In a remote environment, there's less hand-holding: You need to trust yourself to do the work without constant feedback, and you need to speak up when you have questions or ideas; after all, your co-workers and boss won't know you need help until you tell them. Not everyone is comfortable with it. But you do need to know when and how to ask questions. The most important rule: polite, but firm and to the effect.

4 EMPATHY

Working remotely, you have to be able to put yourself in another person's shoes: not only understand the needs of a colleague, colleague or superior, but also step into their shoes without the possibility of live contact. You will have situations where your private life influences your professional life much more often. You then have to throw off the office mask, which for some is not easy, but a part of working in a remote team.

According to a Businssolver report, **60%** of employees would rather work in a more empathy-driven environment than earn more money.

5 ABILITY TO ADAPT

Remote work requires flexibility in all circumstances. Where and when you're working might change, and the colleagues you're collaborating with might be people you've never even met in person. Regardless of surprises or challenges, the key is to be willing and able to adapt to changing circumstances.

6 GOOD COMMUNICATION

Effective remote workers can communicate very efficiently. In the remote work community, it is often said that too much communication is better than not enough. This is true, but you need balance and a sense of context. Are you scheduled to see your doctor several times that could affect your working hours? Let the team know in advance about your unavailability. Are you late with the project because you are waiting for an external supplier? Send your co-workers a short note. Purposeful communication – clear, well thought out, and informative – is essential to successful remote work. (More on this in Chapter 6!)

7 SELF-ORGANIZATION

Employees who can effectively manage their work find it much easier in a virtual environment. Being a good self-manager is essential – whether we are talking about the ability to analyze situations independently, be involved in preparing an action plan, communicate progress or problems, or take full responsibility for results.

CHECK WHAT TYPE
OF PERSONALITY YOU HAVE

There is no single recipe for effective work outside the office – everyone has to find the mode best suited to their needs and character. *When am I being most productive? How should others communicate with me? What tasks are most fun or interesting for me?* Remote work is the perfect excuse to get to know yourself better.

And of course, "there is an app for that" – an online test developed by the Wall Street Academy.[13] Filling it in takes about 10 minutes and allows you to determine the type of personality, capturing its most important features. The results may surprise you! I encourage you to take this or other personality tests to take stock of yourself. The results can be a useful point of reference and may help you better understand how you can utilize the advice that will come in the next section of this book. It will be easier for you to adapt the presented tips to learn how to work remotely as comfortably as possible.

FIRST-HAND

Dorota Piotrowska

A long-time manager of human resources and development for agile, inclusive organizations and remote teams, Piotrowska serves as an advisor to tech startups and a Future of Work expert.

I became a remote worker the very same day I became Head of People at Netguru, a remote first company, so my personal journey to becoming remote smart was very much intertwined with me doing my best to strengthen the cultural underpinnings and the routines and rituals of team collaboration and communication conducive to a healthy, productive remote first workplace.

I quickly realised that trust and transparency will make or break our remote organisation. I could quickly tell how trust and empowerment are the flip sides of ownership and accountability, as well as blame free, innovative culture so critical for today's increasingly more and more knowledge based and digitalised economy.

Our leadership team realised very well that feedback is one of the key pillars of trust and that the ability to give, take and solicit timely, honest, caring, constructive feedback, to seek disagreement in order to expand options and ensure inclusive debate, are all critical for our, or any other remote smart teams for that matter.

We made sure that all new joiners learned about the power of radical candor during their first onboarding day (so grateful to Kim Scott for her great Radical Candor book), and that all our leaders were properly trained to be the role models and to coach on how to give, take and solicit feedback from their peers as well as direct reports and executive leadership team. Feedback was in the DNA of the company, practiced through very many After Action

Reviews, results of which were transparently published for everyone to learn, through quarterly performance feedback sessions where every individual employee received 360 feedback and was encouraged to give feedback to their direct leader and to the company's executive team, through AMA sessions with the leadership team and many other org wide or team rituals.

Feedback was at the foundation of things. And we all had to learn the HOWs of it, and to commit to exercising the feedback muscle on a daily basis in order to ensure that despite limited access to non-verbal language typical for asynchronous or online communication, and despite cross-cultural differences we'd all feel we belong to a community that cares about each-other's professional and personal, as well as about company's growth.

FIRST-HAND

Magda Sowierszenko

As co-founder and Head of Marketing and Communications at Remote-how, Sowierszenko is an expert in the fields of communication, marketing and project management and specializes in organizing virtual conferences and trainings.

If you're anything like me, when you hear the word "networking" you're feeling sick and your stomach turns upside down. Chances are, you might be the kind of person who prefers establishing deeper relationships over meeting a dozen strangers. Does it mean, you won't be able to thrive at remote work and you'll never build strong bonds remotely? No! Quite the opposite.

Over 3 years of my remote work experience, I've learned that it all boils down to "being Intentional". While working with remote teams, you have to be intentional about communication and collaboration. While leading the whole remote company, you have to be intentional about the culture and values. Same goes for building relationships with your co-workers, clients, vendors, and many other stakeholders you encounter in your daily work.

Yes, you got it. You have to be intentional about it.

Start small. Pick people, who you'd like to meet them better. When you meet virtually, start noticing things you have in common and what's important for them. If you'll get a chance, when you meet them next time, recall this information. You'll see it makes "awkward" beginnings of the meetings much easier, and more natural. Especially if you meet with these people on 1-on-1s.

Remember to make others feel good and appreciate them often. One tricky part though, it must always be honest! You can easily make it your habit to thank someone for their work. It won't only impact your relationships with those around you, but it will also provide many physical, psychological and social benefits to your virtual workplace!

Lastly, make sure to help others, whenever you can. Sure, it's easier to hide away in your home office and not answer someone's call for help, but just give helping others a try. As a general rule, it's important for relationships to give something from yourself, and in work that often means doing someone a favour, or helping them out. You have to make the effort. You have to get intentional about it.

With time, you'll notice, growing a network of people you really enjoy connecting with and your work relationships will improve. Practicing for over 3 years got me to a place where I can confidently say that I have a strong network of Partners, remote work experts that I can confidently reach out to when I'm in need. And you know what's the best?

I haven't met 80% of them, and I still feel closer, much more comfortable with them, than with many people I used to work with in a regular office, a couple of years ago.

CHAPTER 5:

REMOTE-FRIENDLY COMPANIES

MORNING COFFEE: KOZIA GÓRKA, POLAND

It's May 2018 and I'm at place I've been coming back to for 22 years: a former forester's lodge in the middle of nowhere, just outside of Łeba, Poland's popular seaside summer spot. Kozia Górka – which translates in English to the less-romantic-sounding Goat Hill – is an oasis of peace. It is May 2018. Preparations for the first Remote Future Summit are entering their final phase. I sneak out of the bedroom and go upstairs to make coffee. I press "Start" and … water starts to trickle from under the espresso machine onto the wooden floor. Not again! My parents, who own this vacation home, were supposed to have this fixed ages ago. But they're always better with big ideas than dull practical tasks – hey, where do you think I got that same trait from?

I take my laptop and mug and go outside. A sun-drenched lake, wrapped in birch trees, appears before my eyes. I breathe in the fresh forest air and move toward the pier. I'm not alone – Kendra, my mother's best canine friend, joins me. I open my computer to join the virtual office … and enter a world of mild chaos. Conference planning is going great, but the team has ballooned from 3 to 14 people and we're working out the kinks as we power forward. At the same time, I've been trying to direct renovations on our apartment in Gdańsk from afar, but having trouble getting several teams of contractors and workers to do what I need them to do. I can clearly see the shortcomings of our distributed management model. And yet there are companies that do it well and their employees are satisfied. Time to find out their secret. I open the first e-mail and Kendra puts a long doggy face in my lap, demanding to be petted.

SOME COMPANIES UNDERSTAND

It was only after the outbreak of the COVID-19 pandemic that many companies realized that remote work was the future. Over the years, most have remained impassive, despite numerous studies proving remote work's merits, both from a purely financial point of view and due to increased employee satisfaction. Change came almost overnight, with the most influential technology companies in Silicon Valley as an example. One by one, they took steps to become remote-first, and the summer of 2020 brought a flood of reports about modifying the remote work policy. Such giants as Facebook, Twitter, Shopify, Square or Spotify – enterprises with a total value of $800 billion – have announced the implementation of various forms of remote work in post-pandemic reality. The revolution has become a fact.

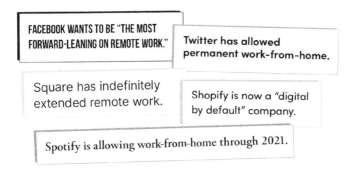

FACEBOOK WANTS TO BE "THE MOST FORWARD-LEANING ON REMOTE WORK."

Twitter has allowed permanent work-from-home.

Square has indefinitely extended remote work.

Shopify is now a "digital by default" company.

Spotify is allowing work-from-home through 2021.

WHAT DO COMPANIES GAIN FROM REMOTE WORK?

Remember all the "why not" arguments you heard from your superiors when you raised the subject of remote work? Neither the global increase in the number of freelancers, nor the dynamic development of technologies for remote work, nor the now-ubiquitous presence of high-speed Internet around the world would convince them. Even such a serious business problem as the shortage of qualified employees on the local market was not able to convince managers to work from outside the office.

It was only the coronavirus pandemic that left employers no choice. "Does remote work make sense?" turned into "How to cope with the new reality?" Office conservatives had to revise their views and finally see that companies around the world have been working remotely for years and are successful. Why is this happening?

Advantages of remote teams

59%	Happier employees
57%	A more global talent pool
52%	More productive employees
40%	Lower office costs for the company
26%	Better employee retention rate

Managers think that the biggest advantages of remote teams are **happier employees** (59%), **a global talent pool** (57%), and **more productive employees** (52%).

Source: Remote Managers Report 2021, autor Remote-how

1 ACCESS TO GLOBAL TALENT POOL

As GitLab CEO Sid Sijbrandij and Automattic founder Matt Mullenweg have emphasized many times, one of the reasons for the rapid development of their companies was the possibility of hiring employees from anywhere in the world. They realized that talent and intelligence were scattered across the globe, but access to job opportunities remained very uneven. Contrary to the traditional competition, companies employing remotely have never complained about the lack of candidates. Everyone was talking about a "talent shortage" while they hired people from around the globe without having to pay recruiting firms thousands of dollars to find the right person "to fit in at the office". They received thousands of applications for one position, so they could choose employees who perfectly matched their teams.

2 INCREASE EMPLOYEE PRODUCTIVITY

Almost all of us have heard: "I have to finish an important project today. I will be working from home so I can focus. " It's absurd: after all, this office was supposed to be the best place to work! Before the pandemic, doubts about the productivity of working from home were one of the most common arguments raised by its opponents. However, hard data from research proves that working remotely is effective. 85% of companies say that switching to remote work has increased their productivity.[14] A Stanford University study of 16,000 employees at CTrip, the US-listed Chinese travel tycoon, showed a 13% increase in productivity in the nine months of switching to work from home.[15] Meanwhile, a study of retail giant BestBuy revealed a 35% increase in productivity as a result of the permanent implementation of a flexible working model.[16]

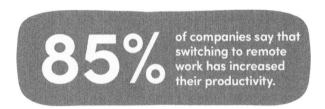

85% of companies say that switching to remote work has increased their productivity.

3 HEALTHY AND HAPPY WORKERS

Numerous studies carried out even before the pandemic – that is, under normal conditions of remote work – show that greater freedom in choosing a workplace has a direct impact on our satisfaction. The data presented by the Polish branch of the Royal Bank of Scotland during the Remote Future Summit 2019 shows that after introducing the possibility of remote work, employee satisfaction, measured by an internal indicator, increased from 72 to 90 points, which is a result of 21 points higher than financial industry average, according to Willis Tower Watson's 2019 report. Meanwhile, a full 89% of workers believe that flexible work options would help them to take better care of themselves, and 77% say it would improve their health.[17]

89% of workers believe that flexible work options would help them to take better care of themselves, and 77% say it would improve their health.

4 INCREASE EMPLOYEE LOYALTY

The average cost of recruiting a new employee ranges from six to nine monthly salaries.[18] A lot! No wonder that companies care about retaining proven people. And greater flexibility in where and when they work is a key way to increase their level of satisfaction. It's going to be increasingly important to turn to remote work as a way to keep your best people on board. Some 76% of employees say they'd be more loyal to the company if they were trusted to work remotely. And 74% say they'd quit their current job if a remote-friendly gig came their way.[19]

76% of employees

say they'd be **more loyal** to the company if they were trusted to work remotely. And 74% say they'd quit their current job if a remote-friendly gig came their way.

5 COST OPTIMIZATION

The final argument in favor of remote work is the possibility of significantly lowering operating costs as a result of reducing office space. I have already mentioned Automattic, which closed down its San Francisco office. In Poland, the Royal Bank of Scotland announced that thanks to the optimization of office space, it was possible to reduce real estate costs by 12.5%, which translates into savings of $2.5 million per year. Research from Global Workplace Analytics in the USA shows that if employees were able to work remotely for at least half of the time, companies saved about $11,000 per year for each employee.

TYPES OF REMOTE COMPANIES

I hope that among so many arguments, everyone will find one that will finally convince them to work remotely. Feel free to use them in discussions with nonbelievers! And remember that objections may arise from the lack of awareness that remote work has very different faces. In our global study titled "The Remote Managers Report 2020," conducted by Remote-how among the leaders of teams working in a distributed format even before the pandemic, the largest numbers were completely remote companies, i.e. all-remote. Hybrid teams belonged to the minority at that time, but that's now changing dramatically as once-skeptical companies open up to remote work. They can choose from a wide range of remote organization types.

Types of Remote Reams

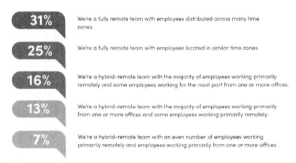

31% We're a fully remote team with employees distributed across many time zones.

25% We're a fully remote team with employees located in similar time zones.

16% We're a hybrid-remote team with the majority of employees working primarily remotely and some employees working for the most part from one or more offices.

13% We're a hybrid-remote team with the majority of employees working primarily from one or more offices and some employees working primarily remotely.

7% We're a hybrid-remote team with an even number of employees working primarily remotely and employees working primarily from one or more offices.

More than half of managers work with teams that are fully remote (56%), and half work with different types of hybrid teams (44%).

Source: Remote Managers Report 2020, autor Remote-how

In our report, we distinguish four main groups of companies that have adapted to remote work to a different extent.

1. All-remote unlimited

Companies that are 100% remote, dispersed in very different time zones.

Examples: GitLab, Doist, Buffer, Zapier, Automattic

2. All-remote with limitations

Companies that are 100% remote, with employees clustered in one or more adjacent time zones.

Examples: TaxJar, Close, GitHub

3. Hybrid

The combination of working from the office (with the possibility of remote work) and working 100% remotely. Examples: HubSpot, Atlassian, Shopify

4. Novices

Companies that started their adventure with remote work as a result of a pandemic. In 2020 and 2021, work took place mainly remotely, but the future is expected to bring employees to transition to the hybrid model.

THE FUTURE IS NOT REMOTE – IT IS HYBRID!

As the results of the research cited earlier show, most of us will prefer to combine remote work with office work. The offices will survive, but in a different form than before. For most employees, they will become a space for meetings and cooperation, including workshops or brainstorming sessions when people prefer to do them live and in person. Some of us will want to work in them every day.

Companies will finally have to take into account the fact that we have different needs. Those companies who want to offer the most flexible options may turn to the hybrid model. But what does it mean?

In such an enterprise, employees are free to work either in the office or remotely. This could mean a model of working three days remotely and two days in the office; it could also mean setting your own schedule but staying within driving distance of company headquarters. Whereas the set-up of all-remote is pretty clear, the set-up of a hybrid team can vary widely. Some ways of doing it might be:

- **Remote optional:** Work in the office most of the time, with the option to work from home when convenient or when not disruptive to workflow.
- **Remote preferred:** Working outside the office is the norm and encouraged, but office space is maintained for specific meetings or activities, or for the benefit of those who prefer a structured workspace.

- **Limited office:** Office use is strictly limited to certain essential people or for certain sensitive tasks.
- **Satellite offices:** in addition to a main office, smaller workplaces in a variety of locations are made available for use to any workers who are nearby and want the option.
- **Rotational office:** Teams A and B work from the office on some days; Team C and D work from the office on other days.

This set-up is slowly becoming the standard. However, at stake with this change is not only employee satisfaction; it also affects other areas of their lives and the company's operations. Happiness, productivity, and overall job satisfaction are just some of the things positively influenced by the ability to perform duties remotely. Having given it a chance for a better life, we must ensure that this new working environment turns out to be truly sustainable.

This is not an easy task, so let me emphasize: if your company or team is not ready for the new model of cooperation, you could spiral into failure. This is especially true of the transition to a hybrid model, which offers more choice ... but also more room for error. What makes its introduction so challenging?

- How can hybrid workplaces maintain and develop a consistent company culture?
- How can they retain workplace transparency?
- How can they make teams feel confident in their daily routines?
- How should they standardize communication?
- How can they centralize mission- critical information for the entire company?

- How can managers keep their teams on track in a virtual environment?
- How can you recognize success – and guarantee equal opportunities for advancement?

Effective leaders of hybrid teams are able to combine remote and office reality, creating an environment in which:

- there is equality and everyone feels part of the team
- the culture of the organization is more than an empty slogan in the "Career" tab on the website
- expectations towards employees are clearly formulated and respected
- Every employee knows what's going on with the company, beyond their own job

All these issues must be taken care of and procedures to be implemented, but – perhaps more importantly – they must be followed on a daily basis. Consistency is the key to success.

PREPARING COMPANIES FOR REMOTE WORK

During the Remote Future Summit 2020, we asked over 3,300 people from HR departments and management staff of companies all over the world about the greatest challenges related to remote work. Maintaining the organizational culture turned out to be their

Number 1 issue – it was indicated by 61% of representatives of HR departments and 58% of managers. Not a day goes by without this issue being raised in discussions with companies that turn to Remote-how for support.

Unfortunately, it often turns out that this problem is not the result of switching to remote work. The change of work mode amid the pandemic simply reveals the existence of problems that these companies had to begin with.

The organizational culture, or "the glue that holds the company together", is the set of values, norms, rituals and features that make it unique. To quote the father of modern management, Peter Drucker: "culture eats strategy for breakfast". The culture of the organization should be cared for on a daily basis – it affects more than just the level of satisfaction and commitment of employees.

Many companies haven't paid enough attention to it. But this momentous shift to remote gives us a new opportunity to turn the spotlight on building and maintaining a healthy, effective company culture.

Here are a few things you should pay special attention to.

1 COMPANY VALUES: EVERYDAY, NOT ON PAPER

The discrepancy between the lovely, flowery description of the company's values as described on the "Career" page of its website, and how those values do or do not manifest in reality for the company's employees and projects is very common. According to Harvard Business Review, only 28% of employees strongly agree that a company's values go hand in hand with its actual actions.[20]

Many companies face immense work in redesigning their inner culture. It is best to learn from those who have already succeeded – including some of the most experienced companies in the world of remote work. That success is reflected in data about their staff. Employee retention is an indicator of how many have stayed with the company over a period of time – often one fiscal year or more. According to leading recruitment portals Monster.com, retention should be around 90% in well-functioning enterprises. Top remote-first companies meet this condition, and often exceed it:

- **Buffer** – 94%[27]
- **GitLab** – 85%[28]
- **BuySellAds** – 90%[29]
- **Zapier** – 94%[30]

Let's look at companies that implemented a hybrid model even before the pandemic. According to Comparably, as many as 83% of HubSpot employees would not leave the company even if they received a higher salary offer from another company, and 91% are excited by their daily work. As many as 90% believe that the company is doing exactly what it should to stop them. [21]

2 TRANSPARENCY AND TRUST

The remote revolution means a break with the current method of management, which is often based on ad hoc activities or micro-management – and thus with the mentality that managers need full control of an employee, and not only the effects of his work. Remote work needs the opposite of full, obsessive control – it thrives when there is a high level of trust between manager and team. According to Great Place to Work, it exists when employees believe that:

- management is trustworthy
- employees are treated with respect
- rules and policies in the work environment are fair

> **Employees at companies with a high trust culture were 50% more productive.**

Can you imagine a better reason to drastically change the type of organizational culture that dominates today? These days, it's not just salaries that lure in the best job candidates – there's an increasing interest in benefits. The famous offices of Google and Facebook, offering on-site perks like free laundry, free 24-hour food buffets and yoga lessons, are a perfect example of this. However, such amenities are not the key to creating a friendly organizational culture. Yes, they can be an element of it, but the basis is an atmosphere of mutual trust.

In companies where high levels of trust are the norm, there are fewer issues with transparency, confidence and honesty. One of the flagship examples is the aforementioned Buffer, operating according to the principle of "default transparency" in many areas. It is based on four pillars:

- full transparency of salaries, revenue, and end-of-year reports
- sharing data on inclusiveness and diversity among employees
- making the code of your open source application widely available
- insight into the product development map.

> Transparency results in trust which is the basis of good teamwork.

This statement by Joel Gascoigne, Buffer's CEO, has been the company's guiding principle from the outset.

3 LEADERS NEED TO CHANGE

After working with thousands of managers from all over the world for years, we at Remote-how came to a conclusion: Management is the key to the whole remote work puzzle. This might seem obvious, but it took time and effort to really whittle away to find the root cause of dysfunction in workplaces that were struggling.

It is impossible to create a friendly virtual work environment without very active support of the management staff. The data presented by Gartner after the outbreak of the COVID-19 pandemic is all the more alarming: As many as 78% of HR department heads believe the greatest threat to successful implementation of a hybrid remote model isn't a lack of skill – it's the attitude of managers.[22]

78% of HR department heads say managers' attitudes are what make or break the success of a shift to remote work.

Long before the pandemic, it was the managers who opposed the implementation of remote work the most. The fear of putting more control in the hands of employees was paralyzing for them. Key hurdles included:

- micro-management and continuous control of employees
- problems with setting clear goals
- failure to support employees' professional development
- lack of transparency of activities and communication
- the prevalence of overtime work.

We already know how important trust is in the functioning of the company. Managers have the most to do here. Many of the differences listed below are universal, and apply to working both inside and outside the office. Unfortunately, office culture has perpetuated many bad habits, and eradicating them will be a long and complex process.

CHANGE FOR THE BETTER

The abrupt transition to remote work mode was a leap into the deep end for most companies. After the initial shock and dealing with such essentials as giving all employees access to laptops or delivering desktops to their homes, companies faced much more serious challenges. Creating an environment that meets remote-first requirements will be a long-term, multi-stage process. Matt Mullenweg, the aforementioned founder of Automattic, put it very interestingly in the "Five Levels of Autonomy". He ranked the degrees of advancement of distributed work, guided by the degree of independence that the company gives its employees in its performance.

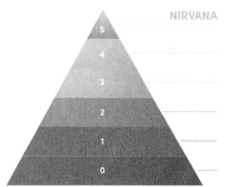

NIRVANA — Work is done better remotely, productivity is at a peak, work-life balance is healthy

5 — High-level remote: Tools, processes, and policies enable smooth functioning for a distributed team

4 — There is a commitment to remote work and investment in systemic changes to aid it

3 — Remote is an option, but workplace processes and culture hasn't changed to accommodate it

2 — Remote is an option, but no action has been taken to make it possible

1 — Work can only be done in person and on site

0

THE FIVE LEVELS OF AUTONOMY

Source: Matt Mullenweg, "Distributed Work's Five Levels of Autonomy"
https://ma.tt/2020/04/five-levels-of-autonomy/

LEVEL 0

Duties cannot be performed without being physically present at the workplace. Examples of such professions include: cashier, policeman, factory worker or dentist. In this case, unfortunately, we cannot do much to increase the availability of remote work. Not yet.

LEVEL 1

Here, there is work that theoretically (and practically) could have been done remotely before the pandemic. This applies to companies whose employees performed their duties online, but could only work from home in special or emergency situations, such as a child's illness or a plumber's visit. Otherwise, work was done at the office. Most companies were operating this way before the pandemic. .

LEVEL 2

This is where you find the novices in the world of remote work, who after the first few months of the pandemic began to realize that they would be working in this mode for quite a long time. The problem is that office habits have been transferred to a virtual environment – often without any changes. Things that worked in the past are being forced into a virtual world, whether or not they fit. For example, there's an over-reliance on synchronous (i.e. in the moment, real time) communication, and face-to-face meetings, rather than finding new or creative ways to do things.

LEVEL 3

Companies at this level are starting to make conscious decisions towards becoming truly remote-work friendly. This means both investments in work-from-home equipment and the first moves towards systemic changes. In the area of communication, for example, there is a conscious reduction in the number of meetings in favor of written messages, and less pressure for immediate, real-time responses. If meetings are necessary, they are thoroughly prepared and the right tools are used to make them successful.

LEVEL 4

This is a very high level of initiation. In such companies, work is judged by results, not by who has been in a virtual office for how long, and communication becomes decidedly asynchronous. Remote cooperation is very well organized: meetings are planned following virtual best practices and tasks are appropriately delegated. The company culture supports the healthy integration of work and personal life. It is also often a stage of development when the company becomes ready to hire people from outside the "typical recruiting region" so far.

LEVEL 5 – AKA REMOTE NIRVANA

An almost perfect world: work is done much better in a virtual environment than in the office. The productivity and job satisfaction indicators are at levels never seen before. Everyone not only knows what to do, but also does it in an optimal way. Moreover, everyone has enough free time to invest in himself, devote herself to his hobbies or take care of their mental health. Work becomes a pleasure..

FIRST HAND

Marek Grygier

The COO and co-founder of Remote-how is an expert in the field of mobile commerce and loyalty marketing. He specializes in the effective organization of work in a remote environment.

Every company has its own culture, whether it is aware of it or not. Figuring out a workplace's true character and what suits it best can be challenging. In our first few years of existence, Remote-how's rules of communication and cooperation have evolved. It has been trial-and-error – we'd implement a new way of doing things, then abandon it after a few weeks as we determined what worked (and what didn't).

Here, I have compiled a few principles that work for Remote--how. Remember that every company is different, so they may not all fit your situation. But as they've worked well for our small, fully remote team, they may be useful or inspiring to you.

1 TRANSPARENCY

In our case, transparency manifests itself in three main ways:

- **financial** – once a week a report is published containing the current structure of revenues, costs and the current balance of the company's account;
- **communication** – we avoid private conversations regarding current projects, all such discussions are conducted in open threads;
- **organizational** – we inform others on a common channel every day what we will be working on that day, and after the end of the day we write what has been done and what has not been done.

2 CHOOSING THE RIGHT MEANS OF COMMUNICATION

In the world of remote work, we often divide forms of communication into synchronous (in real time) and asynchronous (not simultaneous). At Remote-how, we try to handle as many things as possible asynchronously, saving real-time communication for urgent matters. Still, we do prefer to meet via videoconference, which provides us with a space for casual chats and a way to make sure we're all on the same page..

3 THE "AD HOC STOP" PRINCIPLE

This rule is partly related to the previous one, because it requires thinking about the situation and choosing the appropriate form of communication. It means no off-the-cuff calls and meetings. Instead, we make sure virtual meetings are done in an orderly manner, with an agenda and advance planning, so that participants are prepared.

4 THE "ASAP STOP" PRINCIPLE

In the past, we'd get so excited about a new task or project, we'd want to jump on it as soon as possible. But demanding too many things ASAP leads to disorganization, and neglect of other responsibilities. Now, we make sure the only things we deem "ASAPs" are things that really do need immediate attention.

5 EQUALITY

Regardless of role, everyone at Remote-how is treated the same. Everyone has the right to comment on any matter and everyone's input is taken into account when making decisions.

We have more of these types of rules in Remote-how, but the five I've listed here are the ones that I consider particularly important for our team as individuals and the company as a whole. Why? Each of them has a positive effect on our well-being. Thanks to the principles of transparency and equality, we do not feel left out, misled, or mistrustful. Principles of adequate communication, "AD HOC STOP" and "ASAP STOP" are methods that help reduce unnecessary stress and create a more stable workplace.

FIRST HAND

Barbie Brewer

A former Vice President of Talent for Netflix and Chief People Officer at GitLab, Brewer is a Silicon Valley HR expert whose 20 years of experience also include work with giants such as IBM and Cisco. Today, she manages the HR department at Sprout Therapy..

As we have all lived through the 2020 health crisis, I have had time to reflect on the value of remote work for myself and those with similar experiences. As you have read, there were great reasons not just to "allow" remote work, but to thoughtfully find ways to make it the new normal in these difficult times.

I know 2020 has been hard for most people, but 2016 and 2017 made 2020 look like a cakewalk for me. Back then, I was enjoying a successful career at Netflix that came with a daily 180-minute commute and extensive international travel. Unfortunately 2016 also included a divorce that would make me a single mother every other week. I had to evaluate my priorities, and suddenly those demands no longer worked for me.

Then came 2017. I was diagnosed with cancer and spent the entire year enduring chemotherapy. As I wrote letters to my children for each life milestone they would experience, in case I wouldn't make it that long, the decision I needed to make became clear. I needed to focus more on my family, my health and what truly matters. (I don't cry often, but I definitely cried while writing those letters. I have saved them but am thrilled I'll be able to hand them to my kids.)

Remote work was not a "thing" in 2017. I thought my career was over, so took a different track in opening my consulting business. But guess what? That required travel as well – coast to coast in the United States, and even to India. Gitlab entered my life at the perfect time! By the time I joined, they had about 150 employees and were 100% remote. I really never thought I would find a role that would let me work remotely. I was very fortunate that role found me.

I had the pleasure to work with amazing people from around the world, all with different circumstances that made that the right choice for their life. Some were grappling with physical or mental disabilities; others were military spouses who had to relocate often. Some people just preferred it. Most importantly, it came with a new way to gauge career success: achievement was about what you did, not when you did it or how many hours it took.

I have never been happier that I could continue my profession with no borders! I can finally coach the soccer team and still have plenty of time to get my job done. I can take my dogs on a walk or meet up with friends in the community for lunch. I thank Gitlab for that opportunity, including all that I learned from working with the amazing team.

PART 2:

OVERCOMING THE CHALLENGES OF REMOTE WORK

● ○

By now, I'm guessing you've convinced yourself that remote work is what you want, and you can't wait to start taking full advantage of the opportunities it offers. Well, this is probably a good time to bring you back to earth. If you're going to embrace the remote or hybrid-remote future, you have to be prepared for the challenges. That means it's time for a frank, honest conversation about the hurdles you're going to face in the remote world. Because moving from traditional office set-ups to decentralized, future-thinking environments isn't easy. And the fastest way to torpedo your success is by lacking the preparation to deal with those difficulties once they start to crop up.

The research — such as Buffer's 2021 State of Remote Work survey — highlights a consistent list of challenges facing those who work from outside an office environment. That report listed top challenges as collaboration and communication (16%), loneliness (16%) , inability to unplug from work (27%), distractions at home (15%), and staying motivated (12%).

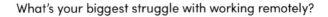

What's your biggest struggle with working remotely?

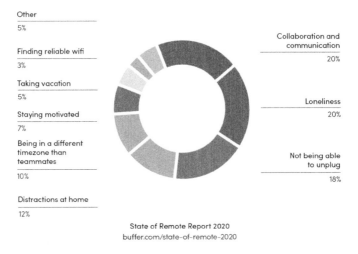

Other
5%

Finding reliable wifi
3%

Taking vacation
5%

Staying motivated
7%

Being in a different
timezone than
teammates
10%

Distractions at home
12%

Collaboration and
communication
20%

Loneliness
20%

Not being able
to unplug
18%

State of Remote Report 2020
buffer.com/state-of-remote-2020

In this section we will tackle these and several other points to help you find a faster path to remote success. However, don't worry too much – proper preparation is the key. There are plenty of strategies and tools to deal with each of the obstacles that may come your way. In this part, I will help you deal with the more difficult aspects of transitioning to a remote world. At first, you'll find it hard to adjust to new communication styles, to stay productive amid an avalanche of distractions, and struggle to manage your time when you don't have the obvious boundaries between office life and home life.

At Remote-how, we've been tracking the data on where remote teams need help since 2017. We analyzed four of the top in-depth studies on remote work – Remote-how's own groundbreaking Remote Managers Report 2020, along with landmark research from Gitlab, Buffer and Terminal – to figure out which challenges and pain points were most common across the board. We found consistency in the struggles with communication, productivity, collaboration, managing teams, and maintaining mental and physical health along with work-life balance. That these issues cropped up across so many reports shows they're not unique, but rather something all remote workers are wrestling with.

With that in mind, I wanted to do more than highlight the problems – I want to be able to offer solutions. In this next section, we'll talk less about theoretical ideas about remote work and instead focus on practical tips that make it easier for you to work outside the office. At Remote-how, we've developed a ton of resources to help navigate these difficulties, and I'm happy to share our recipe for success. The next few chapters are a useful guide both for people who are taking their first steps in the world of remote work and for experienced veterans who've hit a roadblock. I also asked some of the sharpest minds in the remote work world to share their own thoughts and solutions to tackling these problems. But for now, enough talking – let's get to work!

CHAPTER 6:
COMMUNICATION

MORNING COFFEE: SIHANOUKVILLE, CAMBODIA

It's 6 a.m. and the air conditioner in our room just switched off unexpectedly. It's yet another power outage – welcome to life in Cambodia in 2019. It might be early morning and only March, but within a few minutes, the temperature is unbearably hot. Together with Marek, we set out to look for coffee. Finally, we stumble across a place with its own power generator. Miracle! We order two black coffees on ice and sit by the sea. We're nearing the end of our second month here in Asia; the rest of the team is currently spread over eight different countries on three different continents. We're finding that our usual methods of communication aren't enough when we're spread so far. Our efforts to interact asynchronously don't seem to work the way we want them to. Marek is rattling off a few ideas about new strategies we can try to smooth things over when he's interrupted by the noisy appearance of a jet ski on the horizon. We spend the next two hours sorting out a plan for improving our team communication .... then reward ourselves by hopping on a jet ski of our own and zipping around the Cambodian waves.

REMOTE COMMUNICATION CHALLENGES

Research shows a strong positive correlation between communication and how well workers perform: good communication means higher productivity, better decision making and closer teamwork.

And yet, a 2021 report from Buffer[23] found at least 16 percent of remote employees consider communication to be a major pain point, while Remote-how's 2020 Remote Managers report found about 47% of managers were struggling with communication problems.

So why do things so often go wrong ... and what constitutes a solid communication foundation in a remote world?

Your job duties in a remote workplace

Source: buffer.com/state-of-remote-2020

We live in an era of constant notifications and amid a never-ending fear that if we don't process all these drips and drops of information ASAP, we risk falling behind. It's classic FOMO syndrome, i.e. Fear Of Missing Out. This bleeds into our work culture, too – we try to show that we're dedicated and hard-working by staying constantly connected and available, no matter the day or time. One New York-based entrepreneur neatly captured how this cultural imperative affects our daily lives: "I used to wake up and turn off the alarm and check Tinder," he told a reporter for *New York* magazine.[24] "Now I wake up and check Slack."

Research shows that the average Slack user is connected to it for more than 9 hours a day.

Of those 9 hours, only 1.5 hours are spent on active communication.[25] These numbers are overwhelming – 85% of the day we are online in the application is full of breaking the rhythm of our work.

Worse, it doesn't just apply to time spent at work. Imagine the following situation: it's evening, a few minutes after 9 p.m., you're lounging on the couch watching Netflix, when suddenly your phone starts buzzing with notifications. It's your boss. What do you do next? Chances are good you'll pick up the phone and reply. But what if you just ... turned off notifications? Or what if your boss didn't expect you to be available in your off hours at all? The reality for most remote workers, however, is that replying later is not an option. The trouble is, most workplaces haven't bothered to think through their own policies about internal communication. They're not thinking through why such messages are being sent at all – nor why employees are expected to be checking them at all hours.

Both of these behaviors come from habits of synchronous communication: meaning, messages are transmitted and received in real time. Just like a normal conversation: one person says something and expects an immediate response from the person he's talking to. Imagine this in the office. You're scrambling to prep for an important meeting that starts in an hour when suddenly the boss drops by your desk and asks about something that won't be due for another week. Because he's right in front of you, you have an obligation to break away from your meeting prep and engage in the conversation. You politely remind your boss that you're scheduled to discuss the issue later this week at the weekly status meeting. "Oh yeah, thanks!" he says before wandering away. It was just a few seconds of interaction, but that disruption can cost you dearly. According to a study by the

University of California, it can take as long as 23 minutes to get your concentration back to where it was before you were interrupted. [26]

Now, in the remote world, it's not just a person or two dropping by your desk when they're nearby – it's a constant flood of spur--of-the-moment, stream-of-consciousness interruptions piling up one notification at a time. They may seem small or benign individually, but together they turn into momentary thieves, stealing our time and attention.

Patterning our remote-world communication on the habits of in-office interactions is just no good – for several reasons:

- It hurts productivity – for both the individual worker and the team as a whole
- It disrupts the flow of information and can lead to confusion or miscommunication
- It can cause stress and harm workers' mental health

So what's the way forward? The short version is: You're going to need to change the way you communicate. The old ways are out, and there's a whole new set of principles that can guide your individual and organizational communication along the road of remote work. The terrain might be different, but the result is the same: You want to operate in a way that gets you where you're going. Here's how you can do that:

CHANGE THE WAY YOU COMMUNICATE

First, you have to accept that the old habits will not work. In a traditional office environment, physical space is organized to facilitate synchronous communication, and everyone knows roughly when it's appropriate to meet and talk, and when it's not the right place or time. Seeing one another in person every day builds relationships, and sets us up for spontaneous chats that can lead to valuable information sharing and new ideas. Remote teams don't have the same luxuries of presence and physical resources, or even guaranteed shared working hours across time zones.

For these reasons, we need to break some habits and stop relying solely on synchronous communication — meaning face-to--face meetings, phone calls, and the like — and start embracing **asynchronous communication.**

Asynchronous communication allows people to send and receive information at their own pace. Messages go out whenever it is convenient for the sender, but there's no expectation of an immediate reply or reaction from the recipient. Everyone is communicating when it's best for them.

If you're wondering when asynchronous or synchronous communication is the better choice, this breakdown may help:

USE ASYNCHRONOUS FOR ...	USE SYNCHRONOUS FOR ...
Whenever possible!	1:1 meetings
Check-ins or updates	Critical and direct feedback
Group feedback/praise	Tough news (e.g. layoffs)
Non-critical all-hands "meetings"	In general, whenever "ego" is involved or when you have to read between the lines

Source: Remote-how Academy

The top remote-based companies around the world have already fully embraced the asynchronous approach as a pillar of their internal communication strategy. Zapier, for example, has teams publish summaries of their work each Friday; they can be viewed by all employees and they're open for comments and reactions whenever people get to it. GitLab has been so dedicated to refining their asynchronous communication processes that they now boast of an "Asych 3.0" initiative[27], through which they're establishing best practices and experimenting with new ways to talk to one another. Doist's CTO once raved that "the extra time to let things sink in, to think, to reflect, and craft an appropriate response, really pays off."[28] They, along with many others, have selected and developed tools that help their remote teams stay in touch across time zones and work shifts.

Some of this asynchronous culture has already been broadly normalized. Waiting a few days to respond to private messages from friends on Messenger or WhatsApp isn't all that surprising to anyone anymore. There are no written rules – it's just the way we communicate now. But when it comes to the workplace, it gets trickier;

here, the move towards asynchronous communication requires clearly defined rules and expectations.

It's worth the effort, and not just for the sake of productivity. Changing the way we communicate gives us more control over our private lives and more freedom. For example:

- From the company's point of view:
  - Fewer time-sucking, unproductive meetings
  - A smoother flow of internal communication
  - Better documentation, archiving and overall transparency of information
- From the employee's point of view:
  - More room for anyone to participate in important conversations, even if they aren't available when the conversation starts
  - Reduces the pressure to be "always on" and available for work
  - Increases productivity when you ARE "on" for work by allowing you to manage your time effectively

THE GOLDEN RULES OF COMMUNICATION

When it comes to trading information, it's not just about timing. Here are the main things to watch out for in terms of HOW you convey your ideas.

1 KEEP IT SIMPLE

In a remote world full of stimuli, the fate of a message depends on its clarity and brevity. If the messages you send are short and specific, they're more likely to be understood and less likely to lead to confusion, crossed wires and big old messes.

In short, keep it short. Do what you can to remove unnecessary words and whittle things down to their most essential parts. In written communication, instead of launching into long explanations of what needs to be done, consider straightforward, simple instructions or lists of tasks. Instead of weighing all of the options, highlight which ones are best. If you need help with keeping your messages clear and without grammatical or spelling errors, there is an app for that – Grammarly. It helped me ensure everything I write comes across the way I intend.

Brevity may also be beneficial in verbal communication; during online meetings, try not to deviate from the main plot by getting wrapped up in tiny details.

SKIP THIS	SAY THIS INSTEAD
Please do not hesitate to contact me if you have any questions or concerns.	E-mail me with any questions.
I hate to bother you with such minor issues, but if you have a moment could you please help me with the report?	Sorry, can you help me?
In the event you cannot make the scheduled meeting time, please take a moment to suggest an alternative day for connecting.	If you can't make it, suggest a new time.
At the conclusion of the meeting, the consensus seemed to be that Jane would compile a final document for the project. Is that an accurate summary of what happened?	We agreed Jane would write the project report. Is that correct?

2 MOVE THINGS FORWARD

One of the traps of asynchronous styles of communication is that the conversation can easily stall out. This means that you must be firm and consistent in your requests and suggestions. Letting ideas float out there half-heartedly or without a final decision can trap you in a cycle of "circling back to this ..." In a remote environment, you have to speak up quickly and loudly.

Moreover, before ending any meeting, e-mail exchange or chat thread, be crystal clear about deadlines and expectations for next steps. If everyone leaves the virtual table with a clear understanding of what comes next, you're less likely to lose your momentum. When team members are clear on the steps they need to take, it's easier to cut down on noise and focus on the work. Due dates help with prioritization, and flexible assigning allows team members to pass the baton to another.

3 CONTEXT MATTERS

Face-to-face communication and office culture do have the benefit of nuance: tone of voice, facial expressions, body language, and other little extras that can get lost in written asynchronous communication. The flat monotone of text on a page can lead to plenty of confusion and misinterpretation.

You can't assume your jokes will land without an in-person delivery, and need to be mindful of irony and sarcasm, and also shorthand that can be misunderstood without full context. Without the same personal relationships you can cultivate face-to-face, you can risk coming off as curt when you meant to be cute, or rude when you mean to be relevant. Because so much can go wrong here, lean on being encouraging, positive and generous with exclamation points or other markers that make clear things are being said on an up note.

And it's not just about how you write things, but how you read them as well. For as much care as everyone should take in crafting a message, it's worthwhile to take an "assume the best" approach to how you read it. Instead of assuming your colleague took a bossy or brusque tone, consider if it can be chalked up to the speed of the message, or the medium in which it's delivered. Reach out for clarification when you need to, but always approach from the "he didn't mean it that way" perspective until you know more.

Much of this can be alleviated by simply including additional information – explain the hows and whys behind your requests or responses, so people understand where you are coming from. Rather than "Send me the document now," which can conjure up a host of concerns if it isn't ready yet, you can try adding context through explanation: "Please send the document asap – don't worry about it being perfect, I just need to take a look at it for length." Or "I know it's before deadline, but I've got an unexpected meeting to prep for, and even the rough document would help.

#4 CHOOSE THE RIGHT METHOD

So you've got something to say …. But do you say it with an e-mail, a chat, or a call? Do you shout it where everyone can hear it, or target it to specific people on the team? Look to each medium's strengths and weaknesses to decide.

Instant messages – think real-time chats – can be ideal for quick-response interactions, casual catch-ups or check-ins, or any information that doesn't need to be retained or re-referenced at a later point in time. They're more instantaneous, but that pro can turn into a con if the number of chat notifications or lengthy back-and-forths start to get too distracting.

Written communication – think e-mails, company intranet or Slack threads – can let you convey more information, can be easily filed away for reference, and can include links and attachments to additional materials that can be useful. But they lack the same immediacy as chat, as well as the personal connection of a call, and the text-based format can make communicating anything sensitive or collaborative more difficult.

Calls offer the opportunity for real-time bouncing around of ideas, and taking things outside of a text-based environment can make communication more meaningful and nuanced. You'll avoid any confusion about tone, of course. But it's also easier in a vocal environment for people to jump in and out of the conversation while still being heard. There's a more collaborative energy overall, which can pay off if you need to generate ideas or solutions rather than just convey information.

5 VIDEO OR AUDIO?

It can be tempting to just hop on an audio call rather than a video meeting: No need to fear that your co-workers will judge your messy house or catch you with sloppy morning hair if you're just talking and they can't see you, right?

In some cases, it can also be more efficient, and can keep teams from getting distracted by what's on the screen. But you also lose a lot of significant communication nuance: Body language and facial expressions, even via video call, can convey a great deal about how the speaker is feeling and what they really mean. Seeing each others' faces can also lead to better familiarity with who's on the team when you're geographically dispersed. And that face time can eventually build up trust and camaraderie. It's an easy way to nurture remote relationships and help teams feel more connected.

And getting back to our favorite word – yes, *asynchronous* – you may also want to consider ways to use asynchronous video communication to help share ideas across time zones. This could be a pre-recorded video of a meeting participant, which anyone else can view at their convenience. It can help key thinkers be involved in meetings, brainstorms and other participatory events, even when they're inconveniently scheduled. It can also let communication be repeated at will, which can be handy in some situations.

Here are some useful tools for asynchronous video communication:

Loom
Perfect for post-meeting e-mails -- a reply is guaranteed!

Grapevine
Move your daily status meetings and check-ins to recorded video to save time!

6 TRANSPARENCY HELPS

We've already addressed the importance of transparency at length. But I'll raise it again here because it is so closely tied to communication issues. Open, transparent language and feedback can make or break a remote team. Be clear in your messages about what you're doing and why. It also helps to provide quick and clear feedback; if you're afraid to tell someone something's not working, it'll stay wrong. You should also allow an open door to questions and concerns, even in public forums. This level of openness and bluntness might be uncomfortable in an off-line office, but in a remote world, it's a necessity.

Your team members need to trust you to be frank, honest, and reliable in providing them the information they need to do their job and bond as a group. The more information people have, the better able they are to do their jobs. It can also provide a sense of security and a clearer understanding of their role.

Databases or other archives of knowledge can also help give people a sense that they understand what's going on with the company. Easy-to-reference documentation means people can confidently find the information they need, cutting back on endless rounds of question-and-answer messages. They can also be key to on-boarding new team members. The gang at GitLab might be doing this better than anyone right now. Their epic handbook[29] — which would be 10,400 pages of info if printed, and is fully accessible not just to their hundreds of employees but also to the general public — documents company policy, objectives and learning in every imaginable area. It's a major milestone in the area of corporate transparency.

Another solution that can be implemented on messaging platforms, such as Slack, is the use of standardized hashtags. If you create the right guidelines for which hashtags to use and when, it will be super easy to find specific bits of information or portions of discussion. They're just one way to help navigate the massive amounts of information that quickly build up in these kinds of communication platforms.

7 STAY CONSISTENT

As with anything, you need to establish rules so that the mediums and practices that govern your company's communication culture are as efficient and effective as possible. Given the sheer volume of messages you'll get on any given day, find ways to cut out the noise of reply-alls and "thanks" / "you're welcome" detritus that can clog up your communication channels. Consider a company shorthand for which items need immediate response, or how to convey a window of response time — or, just as importantly, if things don't require a response at all. Do whatever you can to prevent duplicating communications across multiple mediums, or overrunning the chains with minor updates and unnecessary follow-ups. Who needs to see this, and who needs to respond? Keep it as simple as possible, and make sure everyone on the team follows suit.

Experienced remote teams do everything in their power to maintain a healthy communication routine. When people engage in bad practices – posting the wrong information in the wrong channel, including or excluding the wrong people, barraging the group with unnecessary or overly-urgent messages – make sure there's a system for kindly but firmly correcting them. For some remote teams, this means documenting special rules for conducting calls or meetings; others have appointed internal ambassadors who ensure that the everyday reality of how people are communicating matches up to the established rules. You don't want the policing to become too burdensome, but you do want to guide people into following the rules after they've been established. After all, keeping communication within the appropriate lines (like, maybe you don't NEED to CC all 12 of those people?) is the only way to keep from making each other crazy.

8 WE ARE NOT ROBOTS

Our world becomes more and more virtual, but one thing remains the same: people are social creatures. Co-workers need to see themselves as something more than machines. It's not just about professional issues — it's about the day-to-day communication that makes a work team a true community. In remote work, where loneliness and isolation are common problems, or where the lifestyle involves constant travel or changes in environment, maintaining a sense of community becomes a critical task.

Remember that each member of a remote team is an individual, with his or her own background, aspirations, and set of challenges. That diversity means one-size-fits-all communication strategies may not work. The pandemic's early days showed that we need more compassion and emotional support in stressful and difficult times. Personal ties are a key part of any healthy remote organization.

From the very beginning of Remote-how, I tried not to create an unnecessary barrier between myself and my employees. Counterintuitively, I've found it *easier* to do this in a virtual space. I want to be the sort of manager who creates a safe, healthy space for my team – a place where everyone feels good and can count on support when they speak up about problems. As a result, I make an effort to be open with them about things within the company and my personal dilemmas. I believe the more we show a human face and not pretend to be "perfect" or robotic, the easier it is to establish sincere relationships with colleagues.

I say we need to break the old rules (within reason) about keeping your personal life out of your professional conversations. This is especially important in the virtual world, where it is easy to fall into a spiral of conversations only about work. Remote employees typically get the information related to their specific projects or tasks .... And little else. With the physical distance and the narrower scope of how they encounter projects outside of their own, the result can be a blindness to how their work impacts other people and other initiatives. One way to solve this is to make sure departments talk to each other, not just to themselves — whether via updates or cross-collaborative meetings. When the communication isn't just about specific needs or demands, it's easier for people to see how their work fits into the whole — and where they can be contributing in ways that weren't previously considered.

There's also a significant need for casual communication that allows team members to connect outside of meetings and project check-ins. What's the new water cooler for casual interactions and knowledge-sharing? In-person, real-time interactions have been critical in the old-school office environment, but recreating them virtually can be challenging. At the end of the day, you want teams spread across the globe to feel like their colleagues are as close as the next desk. That means you've got to prioritize efforts to build and maintain those personal connections. Create ways for people to just be ... well, people, who need to get to know one another, share common ground and points of reference and inside jokes. This can come in the form of a separate channel for casual chit chat, happy hours, or other non-project-related chats and video calls.

9 DON'T IGNORE DIFFERENCES

Diversity is both critical to and a perk of remote teams – but it can come with challenges. Differences in work culture and hierarchies in various parts of the world can lead to communication problems. Consider cultural differences – such as means of dealing with conflict, family and religious traditions, and daily schedules across time zones – when approaching how you communicate something. It could be the root cause of a misunderstanding. And when cultural differences are understood and respected, everyone on the team feels included.

10 STAY POSITIVE

I'll be the first to tell you that I am relentlessly positive, even in the most stressful of times. It's not just because it's in my nature — it's an important way to keep a remote team on track.

Most remote meetings that I run – whether with the Remote--how team or with our external partners – start with a solid dose of laughter. This is where the belief that I am "sunny" comes from: I'm used to infecting others with positive energy. I imagine not everyone loves this trait (even Ola is fed up with my excessive optimism sometimes.) But those positive vibes drive who I am, and how I operate as a team leader, and how I want my team to feel. Over and over I've found that a smile can be a powerful tool, effective even against the most resistant people.

To add a dose of this to your own remote worlds, find ways to communicate positive feedback and to praise each other – managers, colleagues and underlings alike – in a way others can see. Compliments for a job well done make people feel recognized, important, valued, and add to a sense of unity in the group; it's important that these pats on the back don't get lost or overlooked – as they so easily can – in an asynchronous environment.

Try to make a habit of congratulating each other and complimenting a job well done:

- Set up a Slack channel dedicated only to congratulations and positive feedback Dedicate a few minutes of your monthly meetings to give kudos to anyone who went above and beyond, or made a special contribution

- Encourage your team to save these congratulatory messages somewhere so that they can reference them when they're having a hard time

Ultimately, maintaining an optimistic attitude and keeping an upbeat tone in your messages can have a ripple effect in the way people work, how they FEEL about their work, and how they feel about the company. Yes, it takes more effort and energy to put a positive spin on things. But that energy is the glue that will keep a team together through challenges.

FIRST-HAND

Chase Warrington

As the Head of Business Development at Doist, Warrington is responsible for the development of two powerhouse platforms for effective remote work: ToDoist and Twist. He manages the organization of international remote teams, conducts training and lectures, and figures out "what's next?"

People always ask what we're looking for when hiring at a remote-first company like Doist. Culture fit? Definitely. Relevant experience? 100%. World class skills? Duh! But these are the obvious answers, which can apply to any organization. What we really want to see, and who we're really trying to hire, are awesome communicators. I don't mean an army of individuals that can talk to anyone, or never met a stranger – I mean those that know how to do this from a distance, asynchronously.

It's no secret that asynchronous communication is a cornerstone for the most successful remote-first organizations, but what does it mean to be great and asynchronous communication? It takes hiring individuals who communicate via the written form in a very special way. You have to be thorough yet succinct; transparent and inclusive, but mindful of your teammates' attention; timely with your responses but independent enough to be able to wait for a response. It's a delicate balancing act that doesn't always come naturally.

At a company like Doist we screen for this almost above everything else. The very first step in our hiring process involves responding to a series of written questions. Yes, we're interested in what they say – but more importantly, it's how they say it.

I've seen highly experienced professionals apply for entry level positions, and not make it past the CV screening stage – and vice versa. In one such case, an applicant had 10+ years of experience and was applying for a junior position. I was extremely excited about the opportunity to bring on such talent! However, their responses to our questions reflected an inability to deliver a point in a concise manner. After reading paragraphs of business jargon, I still found myself at a loss with regard to what the point was. Meanwhile, a rookie just out of university shined with clear examples and data to illustrate their point, in a matter of a few sentences. Needless to say, we progressed the rookie through the process and politely thanked the veteran for their time.

This is what often separates the good candidates from the great ones, and it's the secret sauce behind our success. We've hired a group of amazing developers, marketers and leaders from 35+ different countries – but the common denominator that bonds us is our communication style. It's that important.

The organizations that learn to harness the power of asynchronous communication will have a substantial headstart on those that try to figure it out as they go.

CHAPTER 7:
PRODUCTIVITY

MORNING COFFEE: DÀ NẴNG

The clock reads 5:56 a.m. in the nearly-empty airport of this coastal city as I order a Vietnamese coffee with milk. It's December
26, 2020, the day after my and Ola's first-ever Christmas outside of
Poland; after celebrating with friends, we're headed to the southern
island of Phu Quoc for a few days. We board the plane of a Vietnamese airline, and are greeted by... a crew made up of fellow Poles.
We are about to spend a few hours in my favorite office: the mobile,
up-in-the-clouds kind. Airplanes have become temples of productivity for me for years, and I'm gearing up to get things done for a
few hours.

PRODUCTIVITY, WHEREVER YOU ARE

Beach, forest, rice field, cafe, port, ferry, airplane, car – these are
just some of the places where I happened to work. Despite the popular notion that the world outside the office is "too distracting," I
will humbly say that in each of them I was usually able to stay focused on my tasks – even if there was a magical view of a Caribbean
beach or the green rice fields of Vietnam spread out in front of me,
or rows of crying babies filling the plane behind me.

So is it possible to be productive no matter where you
work from?

In short: Yes!

Okay, okay, a little longer: Yes ... but only if we can get rid of
two sets of obstacles standing in the way. The first is the problem of

outdated notions of what productivity is and how to achieve it that can't possibly hold up in our new remote reality; the second is the glut of new problems that have cropped up in our modern, always--connected, hyper communicative world to steal our attention.

If we want to be productive in a virtual environment, we need to shift gears so that "productivity" isn't just about churning out quantity, but also quality. In our hyper-capitalist culture, "productivity", "efficiency" and "optimization" are all words meant to be positive, inspirational and good. More, more, more! We should be as focused on our job as possible, with as much tangible output as possible, with every minute dedicated to making money for the company, right? Well ... not exactly.

This type of mentality leads to a humans-last approach to work, at the expense of our well-being and to the detriment of meaningful innovation and satisfying professional achievements. Do we really want to move forward emulating faceless corporate behemoths who haven't changed the ways they do business in decades? Where easily expendable employees toil 12-14 hour days and leave work exhausted and anxious? Where managers end up too busy chasing statistics and the bottom line to address the needs of the people working under them? Where investment in the training and tools that would actually help employees do their jobs better is seen as a costly waste instead of a necessity, or is constantly sidelined in favor of another meeting, client or adherence to a routine?

In our new remote reality, we need to let go of the "more, more, more!" ideals of the past. The 1990s style of work and attitudes about efficiency do not work in 2021 and will no longer work in the future: it is harmful both for employees and for managers and for organizations as a whole. To succeed now and in the future, we need to think about productivity as a means to turning out the best possible product or service, and taking steps toward innovative and interesting output, rather than just checking the boxes and seeing the number of hours work and dollars raked in go up. Let's make it about achievement, not the numbers on a spreadsheet.

Even if we embrace that new vision, how can we stay productive when all the technology that makes it possible for us to work remotely ... is also so very distracting?

These days, we're constantly bombarded by stimuli – notifications flood our phones as cable news banners spell out BREAKING NEWS and a steady stream of pings from every conceivable source keep our brains on constant alert for the next thing to worry about. Trying to focus amid all of this noise can feel impossible, especially when there's pressure to respond immediately. The result is a disorienting pattern of being jerked from one task to the next without full control over what we're doing.

It's a phenomenon that affects us even when the stimuli aren't actually present! According to research by the University of Texas, the phone lying too close alone limits our cognitive abilities and has a negative impact on our work, even if no notifications appear on it.[30]

That same technology is a trap that lures us into a pattern of procrastination. Go on, hand on heart: Who among us has never said: "Oh, I'll just take a break with ONE [Netflix episode / Playstation game / chapter of this book / etc] and then get back to work." Procrastination, the art of postponing what we should be doing, is harder and harder to resist when everything that entertains us is built to tempt us for more.

Add to that the fact that the blurred lines between home and office, work space and social space, now mean stimuli in the real world – family members with a question, delivery people at our front door, baristas firing up a noisy espresso machine – are also distracting our minds from the tasks at hand.

All these distractions are instilling bad habits in us, all of which are compounded by the myth of multitasking. Personally, I've always found it difficult to focus on many things at once. I'm aware of this and tell my colleagues openly that I cannot do two things at once – for example taking notes during meetings. And now, thanks to a number of studies, we know that I'm not the only one: multitasking is an impossible feat.[31] Over and over they show that people who claim that they can do several tasks at once are actually much less productive than if they went about them one at a time. This is how the human brain works, and there is no point in fighting it.

So our challenge to staying productive as remote workers rests in changing both our mentality about what we're trying to achieve, and how we navigate the pitfalls of the very technology and culture that lets us work remotely in the first place.

In this chapter, I will present a set of useful solutions that will change your approach to getting work done. I'll share both my own experiences and hacks for productivity, as well as strategies that are recommended by the best remote work experts associated with the Remote-how Academy and Remote-how's consulting marketplace. Before we begin, however, remember: knowing and implementing are two different things. The key to success is to develop new ha-bits and stick to them; no course or tutorial or tip is going to help you if you never actually implement that advice in your day-to-day life. It requires good organization and being a manager yourself. Unfortunately, not everyone finds self-discipline so easy. But there are ways to make it easier on yourself.

Remember, the goal is not that we should work a lot and all the time. On the contrary! The point is to work wisely and to be acco-untable – especially to ourselves – about the effects of work, not how much time we spend on it.

PRODUCTIVITY STRATEGIES

So how do you overcome these hurdles standing in the way of your productivity when working from home? There are a number of strategies you can take to try to keep you and your work on track. Here, we'll review some of the key methods to stay focused and productive:

1 SET YOUR PRIORITIES

Feeling overwhelmed, and like your mind is hopping from one task to the next without actually completing any of them? It's very pos-sible because you don't have your priorities in check.

When there are a million things to do, it helps to strategical-ly break down which of those tasks, deadlines and responsibilities have to be taken care of first. It instills a bit of discipline and clarity to keep your mind focused on what matters most. Too many to-do items can be a real burden. And trying to do it all at once will only leave you frustrated. Get a clear overview of your most important tasks and gain a crystal clear idea of what has to be done now, and what can be postponed till later. Even if every single item isn't completed, it will ultimately make you more productive and less stressed.

Consolidate all of the information you have into a single place — meaning, pull those e-mails and Slack messages and that scrap of paper you scribbled something down on and that text from your boss and get all of the data in one accessible and unified list. This helps you get a sense of the bigger picture.

Once you have collected all the tasks, you can more easily analyze and organize them, starting with the most urgent ones.

- Be ruthless in determining which tasks you can just ... delete off the top. If it's something that has been bobbing around your to-do lists for ages, maybe it's time to just abandon it. Like true love, if those tasks really matter to you, they'll come back to you eventually. At the same time, consider any items that are valueless chores, more trouble than the payoff is worth, or relics from a past way of doing things .... Just kill them out!
- If something takes 5 minutes or less, do it now. Seriously, don't wait. Because the amount of time you'll spend shuffling it around various lists will all be a waste when you can just knock it out quickly.
- Figure out what you can delegate to others. Does this task really need to be YOUR task? See if it makes more sense for another team member to take it on

Once you've completed these steps, your list should only include specific, meaningful tasks for which you need to establish priorities. Order them from most urgent to least, taking into consideration a) the needs of the company or customers, b) your own preferences and skills, and c) how dependent future responsibilities are on completing these tasks now. Take a closer look at your now-orderly list and see which items are related to each other, and think about how that impacts how you tackle them. Finally, set a deadline for each task.

By the time you are done, it will be roughly clear where to start. And then – let's go! Some people recommend starting with the ones you hate most; others say nibble away at the ones you don't mind, just to make a dent. It will all come down to your own work style. Some of the following prioritization tools and apps may also help you:

Todoist
https://todoist.com/

Atracker
www.wonderapps.se/atracker/

Coach.me
www.coach.me/habit-tracker

GoalsOnTrack
www.goalsontrack.com

Strides
www.stridesapp.com

Trello
https://trello.com/

2 SET A ROUTINE

Developing a relatively permanent routine is very helpful. It creates a mental map, directing our attention and mind to specific tasks more easily.

By following your usual morning routines for getting ready for work (shower, breakfast, getting dressed, make-up), you'll give your mind a signal to get ready for a productive working day. By staying in your PJs all day long, what you're signaling to your brain is that it's a chill day and thus all work tasks will just feel like more of a drag.

So honor the routines and go through the usual steps you might've taken when going to the office: get dressed, listen to your 'work' playlist, have your usual morning coffee…you get the idea.

But that's just half of it! As important as it is to get yourself in the mood for work in the morning, it's exactly as important to wind down and finish the day in the evening.

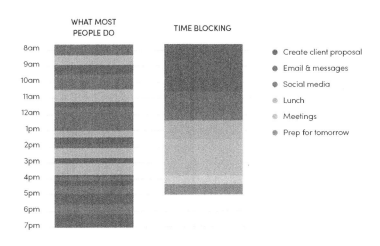

Source: https://todoist.com/productivity-methods/time-blocking

Daily routines are important, because they let our brains do work with less energy. If you have trouble sticking to them, try using an app to keep track of your daily schedule (like Reclaim.ai), or just write down in a notebook what you do at what times.

3 LIMIT DISTRACTIONS

You'll never be able to block out everything, but do what you can to turn off the biggest hazards to productivity. Remove anything from your line of sight that might side-track you in person, but also watch out for those digital or on-screen hasslers. This can mean things like constantly checking your phone for updates, scrolling through social media, pinging news alerts and calendar reminders. Pare down to what's necessary to keep your mind focused.

According to research, checking on social media can reduce your productivity by up to 13%.[32] Mute your phone's notifications and put it away so you don't glance at the screen every moment. If you have an important task to complete, it's best to log out of Facebook, Twitter or Instagram, or even your e-mail inbox. You don't have to keep checking it – how often do you get messages that you absolutely need to reply to immediately, not in a few hours from now? Disconnecting from social media and breaking those must-keep-scrolling habits can help a lot in staying focused. You can also download apps that automatically mute them, such as Justmuteit or Cold Turkey.

Other apps that can help you focus on your work include:

- **Adios** – With this application, notifications about incoming e-mails won't be a constant distraction. You set times when e-mails are received in bulk, and only check them then. I do it every hour, from 8 a.m. to 8 p.m.

- **Serene** – This multifunctional app allows you to create a daily schedule, blocks sources of potential distraction and helps to focus your attention.
- **Freedom** – This service helps you block sites and applications that are most distracting from your work.
- **Noisly** – This one simulates a benign background sound that helps you focus on the task at hand. (I like the sounds of the cafe full of people the most.)

4 TIME FOR A BREAK

Make it a habit to take short breaks every hour. Get up and stretch; look out the window, and if possible, take a short walk at lunchtime – anything to take a break from your current task for a while. Use your breaks wisely: rather than look at a different screen, use the time to disconnect, go get some fresh air – go move around a little. This will help you balance out your energy levels and keep your mind in the zone. Being active can help improve focus when you return to work. Getting your 10,000 steps a day has been linked with improved cognitive performance, and can easily be tracked with most smartphones nowadays. Make sure to try and get some fresh air too. Working from home can often mean that you don't leave the house so often, so take the opportunity to go outside. It will do wonders for your focus and concentration.

Of course, sometimes we have to sit down for hours to get an important project before the deadline. However, you have to be able to set boundaries, especially when you're lacking the usual cues that signal the end of the day (like the departure of your colleagues and the arrival of the office janitor.)

At home, it's a little too easy to keep working long after the usual hours – just relocate to the couch with your laptop and toil away into the night. In the long run, however, you will disrupt your daily routine and take a solid step towards burnout. So let's introduce a small, personal ritual signaling the end of the working day, after which no emails and no slack messages are allowed anymore.

5 CATCH THE FLOW

You'll know you're at your most productive when you hit the workplace equivalent of a runner's high: The flow state.

No, that doesn't mean you're in a chill vacation mindset, or going-with-the-flow in a lazy way. Instead, a "flow state" is when your mind is at full speed, fully focused on the task at hand, and enjoying doing it. You know when you're so deep into a project that you look up and realize hours have gone by in the blink of an eye … and you're enjoying it too much to stop? That's exactly it!

> For me, I get to a flow state by talking to other people. The energy that is generated during meetings drives me to keep working.

Achieving this state is not just about focusing on the task at hand. You also need to defend yourself from things – and people – who can throw you off the beaten track: that means guarding your time and physical space so that you can sink into your work in the best possible way. It can be difficult when someone wants something from you over and over again. My colleague Magda once compared it to oxygen masks on an airplane: You can't help others get the air they need until you've managed to secure your OWN oxygen mask in place. That's really what it's all about: Setting yourself up for success, so that you, in turn, can help those around you succeed.

You can put those protections in place in a few ways.

- Set a schedule of when you're available to interact and when you expect to be alone with your own work. Clearly define the times when you will reply to emails, messages and calls — it could be certain hours of the day, or only on certain days of the week – to limit distractions and give others a heads up on how to manage their time accordingly. Determine when you and your teammates will overlap on work hours, and when things will be asynchronous. A clear definition of when your day in the virtual office starts and ends will make life easier for your colleagues, and for you – taking care of your own work and rest time.
- Sometimes time invested up front can save precious minutes in the long run. For example, if you have repetitive tasks or tasks that could be handed off to other team members, make the effort to document them — in writing, in audio or video recordings, or

however makes the most sense. – here, for example, a tool like Loom comes in handy, for instant video creation, right from the browser window. Yes, it takes extra effort and it's easy to say "Oh, I don't have time for that kind of detail, it's faster to just do it myself." But if you take the time, once, to document the work, you can hand it off easily to others, clearing space in your schedule for the sort of work you really want to be doing.

Once you've got your schedule in sync with your fellow teammates and done away with small but burdensome chores, your mind will have an obstruction-free runway to take flight and catch the flow. And once you're actually in that flow state, you'll find your overall day more productive and satisfying.

DEEP WORK VERSUS SHALLOW WORK

Being productive isn't just about smoothly crossing items off your to-do list. The real goal is to find ways to get down to the tasks that are at the heart of your responsibilities. With a constant barrage of interruptions and distractions, a mountain of small tasks to chip away at, and a lack of focus, it can be easy to work the whole day and still feel like you've completed nothing. That's because you haven't been able to settle into the stuff you really enjoy or the tasks that garner a sense of achievement.

Shallow work is all of those smaller tasks that you nibble away at all day — scheduling, e-mails, message replies, "quick check-ins," minor tweaks to existing materials, updating spreadsheets, compiling routine reports. The sort of stuff that feels like it needs to be done, and makes it *seem* like you're doing useful work, but ultimately leads to maintaining the status quo rather than making real strides forward. It's work that's not particularly taxing mentally, or challenging creatively. It's easy to get trapped in a frustrating cycle of "I'll just finish these smaller/easier tasks and then move on to the bigger ones," ... only to find the routine work takes up your whole day, and you're left back at square one the next day.

Deep work, then, is what really counts. It is a concept refined by professor and author Cal Newport in his book, "Deep Work: Rules for Focused Success in a Distracted World." He describes it as *"professional activity performed in a state of distraction-free concentration that pushes your cognitive capabilities to their limit. These efforts create new value, improve your skill, and are hard to replicate."*

Simply put, it's the work that matters, that gives your job real meaning and influence, that gets your brain churning. If you find yourself drowning in shallow work, the deep work gets neglected — making you less productive, less satisfied and less effective in your role. If you find yourself working long hours with not a lot to show for it, or feel overwhelmed by administrative BS, or if you grind grind grind all day but find yourself scratching your head when someone asks "what did you do at work today?" then you know you're stuck in the shallows and need to make changes to swim for the deep.

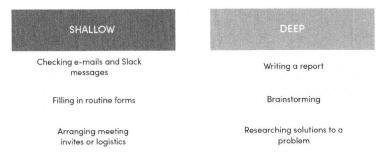

SHALLOW	DEEP
Checking e-mails and Slack messages	Writing a report
Filling in routine forms	Brainstorming
Arranging meeting invites or logistics	Researching solutions to a problem

Source: https://blog.doist.com/deep-work/

Your goal with productivity should be to do more than scratch the surface — it should be to do the best, most advanced work of which you and your company are capable, and to keep growing and learning as you go. This is what deep work is all about – improving the quality and value of what you do, and leaving you more satisfied overall. Newport's full book is worth a read — he's loaded with great ideas — but the central ideas around how to achieve deep work boil down to:

- **Set a structure:** Be strict about when you'll start and stop working, plan ahead about where and how you will work, and be clear with others about your intentions and limits. Give yourself deadlines to create a sense of urgency around tasks or projects, and create a system of accountability to track your progress as you try to move closer to your goals. If you have a clearly defined path, you're more likely to stay on it. And that clarity can also help others around you make better use of your time and their own.

- **Find ways to reduce shallow work:** Crossing a few easy tasks off your to-do list is fun, of course, but it distracts you from your actual responsibilities in the long run. Look at how you are spending your time, and find where you can pare out dull or repetitive activities. Every job will require some degree of shallow work — hey, that's life! And "shallow" isn't the same as "unimportant – many of these things really need to be done, or else everything will fall apart like a house of cards. However, if you manage to automate or delegate some of these responsibilities, you'll have more time to do deep work. Most jobs involve a fairly solid dose of shallow work, but you should try to minimize and contain it as much as possible. For me, this means, for example, reducing the number of meetings with outsiders who want to 'call in' to talk 'about a new project' and focusing on the company's strategic plans, while still keeping these conversations going – but asynchronously.

- **Embrace boredom:** If you're just browsing social media to keep your mind occupied, you better just sign out. This will allow your brain to really relax and create a space to freely develop your own thoughts instead of constantly processing someone else's. The same applies to the time spent with the phone in hand or in front of the screen – these devices that give us access to so much can also slow us down and keep us from getting to the knowledge and effectiveness we seek. Instead of zoning out with Netflix while you fold the laundry, use that time to let your brain get bored enough to work through that problematic work task that's been plaguing you for days. Instead of half-listening to a podcast on your daily run or long car trip, let your mind wander around the things you want to do in your next deep work session.

So how do you conduct a formal deep work session? It's easy!

- Set a date and start/end times.
- Invite colleagues to join (optional)
- Establish clear, attainable goals for the session, and share with participants before it begins
- Turn on a productive Spotify playlist or other background sounds that help you stay focused
- Start the stopwatch
- Work only on what will help you reach the goal you established before the start of the session
- Five minutes before time runs out, remind everyone that the end is near
- Close the session by asking everyone if they managed to achieve their goals, or taking stock of what you achieved yourself
- Schedule the next session right away, rather than putting it off as a task for the future. If you liked it, set it as a recurring event on your calendar.

RE-EVALUATE YOUR WORKSPACE

"Not in an office" can mean a million different places. You have to choose the environment that suits you best. However, if this space is not designed for work, you're going to struggle. Here are some things to watch out for if at-home is your go-to working environment:

1 DESIGN A PLACE EXCLUSIVELY FOR WORK

Not everyone can have the luxury of a separate office at home, but even having a corner of the room or a table intended only for work will help you get the right setting every morning. Working from bed, the couch, the kitchen table can blur the lines with all the other activities that can happen there. If you do not (always) want to work from home, choose a specific café, co-working office or other place that you associate with work, and not, for example, meetings with friends.

2 BRING THE OFFICE HOME

In other words: make sure you have the necessary equipment. Hunching all day over a tiny laptop is a bad idea. Consider whether an extra monitor, keyboard, headphones, or a portable computer stand should be integrated into your home set-up.

3 ERGONOMICS MATTERS

We often underestimate how much the way we sit (or slouch, or lean, or hunch) can impact our physical well-being .... until the back pain becomes truly unbearable. Your body matters just as much as the tech tools; make sure your home workspace is taking care of your physical health. This can mean adjusting the height and layout of your desk, investing in more comfortable chairs, using headphones instead of holding a phone to your ear for calls, etc.

4 SET SPACE BOUNDARIES

In an office there is a sense of propriety about when to invade someone's desk area or private space; at home, those boundaries are invisible to spouses, kids, visitors, pets, delivery men and neighbors knocking at the door. Anything you can do to avoid interruptions and to carve out a work zone that won't be infiltrated by others will help you retain productivity once you're in the zone. It can be as basic as a "do not disturb" sign, or a white noise machine that keeps errant noises out – anything that makes clear you're at work and unavailable. In a co-working or public space, the way to set boundaries may be to put on visible headphones whenever you are in the middle of deep work, to signal that you're unavailable.

NOT AT HOME, BUT NOT AT THE OFFICE

Sometimes we need a change of environment or a more separate space than what we can achieve at home. Or, if you're a digital nomad or any sort of remote worker who travels, you'll need to find ways to mix things up. This can mean working from a variety of external locations, including:

CAFES, COFFEE SHOPS, RESTAURANTS

These can be great places to spend a few hours of productive work with fresh surroundings (and the bonus of highly stimulating caffeine!). The key is to find the spaces that have comfortable tables and chairs, strong, reliable wifi, and that keep the distractions (music, crowds of other patrons, noisy machinery) to a minimum. Of course, it's impossible to completely avoid noise and bustle, which is why I recommend working in a cafe primarily to people who can disconnect from the environment and focus on the task at hand. In turn, your work shouldn't be too sensitive or confidential – when you are in a public place, you can never be sure that someone will hear your conversation or read something over your shoulder. The café is a great place for creative work – changing the environment can be invigorating, especially if you feel too isolated at home.

OUTDOOR SPACES

Parks, gardens, beaches and other public spaces can be ideal in nice weather. So long as you have wifi and a place to sit, why not soak up some Vitamin D while on the job? Much like cafes and restaurants, you need to be wary of the other activities around you, and these are usual spots best for working for an hour or two, rather than full-day marathons.

CO-WORKING SPACES

If you miss some aspects of the office environment, but want to work on your own terms, co-working spaces are just right for you. They are designed for functional, comfortable working and stake their reputations on reliable internet access. They can also be a great way to interact with likeminded people, or other remote workers doing interesting things. Money can be a deterrent for some

– these spaces typically cost more than just a cup of coffee, after all – but the payoff of a productive space can make it worth every cent. If you are wondering how to find the best co-working spaces that suit your needs, try Coworker or Workfrom – they have already done the job for you.

FIRST-HAND

Mark Tippin

As the Director of Strategic Next Practices at MURALOne, Tippin believes that man and his imagination are irreplaceable, and the best results are achieved by combining human resources with technological possibilities.

In the 90's I participated in a multi-day workshop in San Francisco, CA. It was fairly demanding, and as the topics changed, I found myself feeling exhausted at certain points, then feeling wide awake and energized again soon after. I wrote it off to the ups and downs of caffeine and food intake and figured, "that's just how it is."

The next day, I was surprised when our facilitator drew everyone's attention to this very phenomenon. "How many of you are feeling a little tired right now?" she asked. Many of us sluggishly raised our hands. "What if I told you there was a $20 bill taped to the bottom of your seat?" Several folks immediately reached under their chairs. There was no money there. But we were all much less sleepy.

"We often respond to uncertainty with a lowering of our energy level," she explained. "The next time you feel tired, ask yourself what you might be resisting. What isn't clear for you? Do you know what you should do next? How to do it well? Why it's of value to you or someone you care about?" Her point was that "feeling tired" is not always about lack of sleep. Many times our inability to get going on something stems from a mental opposition to some aspect in the moment.

This insight has served me well ever since. When I'm clear on the what, how and why of a task, and I believe my effort will make a difference, then the work seems to flow. I don't struggle with productivity. However, if I'm not sure why I'm doing something, or I really don't know what should be done first, second, third, then I procrastinate.

So why is productivity such a challenge sometimes? First, we often enjoy the moments of "flow" without taking time to better understand the conditions that enabled those moments of clarity, creativity and productivity. Conversely, when we're just not motivated, the task just seems impossible.

Why? What might you be resisting?

Asking yourself this question, and cutting yourself some slack for being human, might allow you to see a small step forward. Maybe the focus on the end result obscures the first, simple step? Maybe there's an element of the task that is not aligned with your integrity? Maybe you are just exhausted – but then you are resisting something: self-care.

CHAPTER 8:

COLLABORATION

MORNING COFFEE: CANGGU, BALI, INDONESIA

I just finished my first surfing session. My instructor was a native Balinese who lives permanently in ... Finland. She says she likes snow and frost very much. I remember a friend of mine, a resident of the Arizona desert who dreamed of a rainy Ireland. This is the complete opposite of our motivation. Bali, a hub for remote workers and digital nomads, has tempted us with the everlasting summer. We are fresh from the high of running the first Remote Future Summit conference – but now it's time for a post-mortem. One of the issues bothering us is team cooperation. We successfully coordinated 64 speakers and several dozen partners from all over the world – now it's time to step back and evaluate how we could have done it better. I take my first sip and start brainstorming.

PRINCIPLES OF REMOTE COLLABORATION

Many managers trying to find their footing in the new, virtual reality wonder how to carry out assigned tasks and meet goals without letting the work come at the expense of overtime and employees' health.

Project management in remote teams is a challenge, as it requires both the introduction of new processes and tools, and – most importantly – a change in the attitude with which leaders manage their teams. Good news: it's all worth it! The key is to learn the skills and tools you need to facilitate virtual group collaboration.

Most of the advice in the previous chapter was aimed at helping individual workers be productive and successful. But what about when the work isn't all about you and what you can do? While three-quarters of respondents to a Boston Consulting survey on remote work[33] said they'd been able to maintain productivity on individual tasks once they started working from home during the pandemic, only about half could say they were equally productive when it came to collaborative tasks. And there's the trouble: When the work requires multiple participants and team involvement, there are more ways for it to go wrong.

But why should collaborative work be any more challenging than individual work, if everyone has what they need to do the job? The BCG study mentioned above found that it boiled down to four possible pain points:

- **Team cohesion** – Employees who said they had strong bonds with their colleagues were two to three times as likely to say they were all equally effective on collaborative tasks while remote as they were in the office. However, many respondents complained of missing social gatherings and the spontaneity of face-to-face chats in the office. Without a satisfying way to fill that social gap, productivity suffers on team projects.
- **Mental and physical well-being** – People who reported better mental health during the pandemic were twice as likely to say that their productivity in teamwork had not decreased in remote conditions. A similar correlation was observed in the case of physical health. So it seems managing stress, anxiety and other issues, as well as navigating

the health concerns that come with working from home or in high-stress situations, can greatly impact how teams work together.

- **Work tools** – Those who reported satisfaction with the tools they had to use remotely were twice as likely to report high collaborative productivity. So it's safe to assume that choosing and maintaining the right tools for communication and project management, and providing the proper training needed to use them effectively, can have a notable impact on collaborative output.

RULES OF REMOTE COLLABORATION

Here, let's run through some of the guiding principles that can shape how collaboration works for distributed teams:

1 WHAT ARE WE DOING IT FOR?

Teams are much more motivated if they understand the significance and commercial benefits of the projects they are working on. According to a Kelton Global survey, 87% of employees say that they would like their future employer to be transparent about company actions and decisions.

According to a Kelton Global survey, **87%** of employees say that they would like their future employer to be transparent about company actions and decisions.

So how do you create this openness? First, take the time to explain the "why" behind each project. Explain the business objectives, as well as the technical. Tell me more about why such a decision was made and what impact it will have on long-term goals. If people know the reasons why the project is important, they'll better understand the role they play in getting it to the finish line on time. It is also easier to set priorities and make sure that they are clear to each of the team members. A joint review of key tasks and finding out who is responsible for what will make it easier for you to focus on your work and feel secure that their work is being utilized effectively. It sounds trivial, but unfortunately we're often too busy with our day-to-day responsibilities to pay proper attention to these sorts of things.

2 WHO DOES WHAT?

One of the biggest challenges that remote project managers face is keeping everyone on task. It is easy for individuals to lose sight of what they are supposed to be doing and the end goal of a project when routine is broken, workers are distributed and access to project managers is limited. Managers in an office environment can wrongly assume that just because they can see everyone and ask them "how's the project going?" at any time, that they're in control of what's going on. The same is true remotely, where people struggle with the lack of transparency.

In distributed teams, it is very important to clearly and carefully assign individual tasks to specific people and to ensure that progress is monitored. It's also a good idea to make sure that everyone understands what the expected result is. In a remote team, it is easy to lose focus and veer off the path to meeting project goals. The more specific you are in explaining roles and goals, the more the team will understand what their contributions need to be and the more effective they can be when working from home.

3 COMMUNICATION IS ESSENTIAL

When in doubt, over communicate. Sure, you're probably sick of hearing about how important this is after Chapter 6, but we can't stress it enough. A report by the Institute of Leadership & Management (ILM) says that 88% of remote workers struggle with inconsistent working practices and miscommunication.[34] And poor project communication is the easiest way to kill productivity, engagement, and ultimately results.

With all of the communication, clarity is super important. You want everyone not just to be getting the information, but understanding it clearly and easily. Instructions quickly get confusing when communication is long-winded, unfocused, and lacks empathy. Instead, be sure to choose your words and directives precisely, one task or action at a time. Consider other ways of making things as clear as possible — by showing instead of telling, using visual elements to emphasize key points.

Effective collaboration leverages the strengths of each team member, drives innovative solutions, and builds trust among remote teams. Try to create strategic partnerships within each project. For example, if you have data from customer feedback, pair a Marketing Lead with the Product Lead to develop new customer personas. Hold group brainstorming sessions where all ideas are welcomed and not criticized to inspire excitement and creativity among your team. You will be surprised more than once by how much this can draw in the quieter or more passive members of the team.

4 WHERE DO WE START FROM?

Unfortunately, we very often jump into operational details too quickly and want to rush forward, neglecting to properly introduce everyone to the project. Get everyone on the same page right from the start by making sure your project has an appropriate onboarding process. This could mean lists of necessary materials or tasks, reports and supplemental information for knowledge sharing, compiled data on users or audience, expectations and timelines, and explainers on which tools and technology are expected to be used. Whatever additional materials can help a newcomer jump into the project waters safely.

Consider creating a project roadmap right from the start. This document can help later in assessing whether you are going in the right direction and achieving your goals. Ideally, you should make it collaborative, e.g. in Google Docs, on a virtual board, such as MURAL or Miro, or using other tools. Address questions such as:

- What is your overall goal or the problem you need to solve?
- How will this project help achieve that goal or solve that problem?
- What are the next stages or deadlines?
- Who will be involved in the project? What is each person responsible for?

Having these questions answered in writing, and following up with a kick-off meeting to make sure all participants understand it, will make for a productive beginning. If something remains unclear, be sure to discuss it before you start working. Each meeting participant must feel that they can ask freely and share their observations – until everything is clear to everyone.

5 WHAT DO WE WANT TO ACHIEVE?

Key Performance Indicators (KPIs) help keep the mission on track, and can also be a way to help managers and employees to understand where they're succeeding and where they need help. They'll vary significantly depending on your industry and the job – for someone in sales, it might be the number of new contracts signed or the total dollar amount brought in; for marketing, it might be about site traffic or conversions; for writers, it could be number of words or articles completed. Ultimately, you want to find the questions or gauges that show some amount of forward movement in the work, that can be compared across time or across projects to see when you are doing your best..

> However, don't treat KPIs as micromanagement tools. They should be used to assess progress towards the overall goal.

Make them permanently available for viewing by all team members – be it in an online document or on a specially designed interactive results board. Of course, it is also a good idea to send out regular progress reports – asynchronously of course!

#6 FEEDBACK

Giving feedback, both constructive and positive, is the basis of the success of any team. If you do not notice your employees' efforts, they will feel undervalued, and if you do not pay attention to short-comings or mistakes, they can repeat them endlessly. Many people dislike such situations as they often require going beyond their comfort zone.

> However, it is worth breaking through – honesty strengthens ties in the team in the long run.

It's best to set an example yourself by asking the team for con-structive feedback. This shows humility and sets a tone that seeking feedback shouldn't be scary. In this way, you will be humble and prove that it is not terrible. And for you, feedback can help you to better fulfill your responsibilities and understand how your team members perceive you. It may be unthinkable for many leaders that someone should publicly "criticize" them. However, this is the first step to becoming aware of the problem, as open communi-cation – both ways – is the key to success in virtual environment with the team.

Look for opportunities to give specific positive feedback to your team. This can mean calling out individual achievements in team meetings, kudos e-mails about a job well done, following up on a teammate's suggestion that helped you solve a problem, or any other way to say thanks. But only give feedback when it's warranted: Even the kindest compliment rings hollow when it seems like it is inauthentic or forced.

A good rule is to praise in public, but provide critical feedback face-to-face in private, preferably face-to-face via video chat, or at least by one-on-one call. It's easier to give potentially difficult or critical feedback through conversational communication, rather than via e-mail or chat, because it allows you to deliver it with a clear tone and explanation, and lets the receiver ask questions and get clarification or explain what they need.

If the feedback you give is complex and contains both positive and negative elements, formulate it according to a tried and tested pattern that facilitates its adoption and increases the chances of its implementation:

- **Focus on facts and impacts:** Let them know a specific action they took, what impact it caused, and suggest ways to do it differently next time. "When you did X, the result was Y. Next time, I suggest doing Z instead."
- **Make it open ended:** Let the feedback recipient help you find the solution. "I like that you do X, but it's causing trouble with Y. Is there another way you think we can approach this?"
- **Start and finish with praise:** You can soften the negative feedback with a bit of honest positivity. "I was really pleased by how you handled Problem X! Unfortunately, your plan for Problem Y didn't solve the issue. I see all the hard work you're putting in, and you're

one of the best problem-solvers on the team, so I'm confident that we can find a better option."

You can also create a culture of healthy feedback by involving others. Assign team members in advance to be critical of a task for other team members. This will set the expectation of feedback before the project or task has even started.

7 WE SEE YOU! HOW TO USE VIDEO EFFECTIVELY

Video chat can improve your communication and strengthen your team's bonds. For distributed teams, who lack the non-verbal cues you get from in-person communication, video-conferencing is one of the most important tools. Here are some interesting research findings on virtual meetings at Zoom[35]:

- 95% of people say that video communication has a positive effect on the quality of their work
- 95% believe that it strengthens trust in the team
- 93% agree that using webcams increases the engagement and effectiveness of members of remote teams

Video calls can be an effective way to do daily standup meetings, teach new skills, and stimulate creative brainstorming. Just beware of overuse. Sometimes, "remote newbies" plan too many video meetings in an attempt to simply transfer their old-school office patterns to a virtual environment. Overdoing it can lead to "Zoom fatigue" – that is, the utter exhaustion you feel when you're cueing up yet another video call and you're sick of seeing the same faces in the tiny boxes on screen. In the pandemic age, many of us have just had enough. And no wonder!

If video calls are overwhelming you, try:

- Asynchronous video updates: One-way video updates using tools like Grapevine, All Hands, Remote Workly, or RealTalk can offer the benefits of video without the time pressure
- Speed meetings: Set a timer and talk fast, to add some excitement and keep things from becoming a snooze.
- Walk-and-talks: Switching to audio-only calls for some meetings means I can go for long walks while discussing key projects and ideas. For me, this is a great way to clear my mind and think creatively; walking in laps can also help trigger memory retention. New start-up Spot is a great tool for this, with easy meeting links and automatic transcription of parts of the call.[36]

8 SHARE YOUR KNOWLEDGE

Remote environments create even more barriers for companies to share knowledge with their teams and encourage peer-to-peer learning. A Forbes study shows that Fortune 500 companies lost as much as $ 31.5 billion annually as a result of insufficient sharing of knowledge and competencies! Do what you can to prevent this by identifying subject matter experts and make their skills known to the rest of the team. Give people access to the sources of knowledge they need, both written and in person. This can be a company wiki, channels for knowledge within Slack or Teams, a Trello board, a space in Confluence or Notion or GoogleDoc, that archives key knowledge and learnings, or shared spreadsheets tracking often-referenced data or details. Keep a running list of who does what for each department or project in an easy-to--access place, as well as how that person can be contacted. Encourage team members to document their processes and findings, and to share that documentation in a searchable way that can be referenced in the future.

At the end of a project, remember to document a written summary so that the lessons learned during the experience are not forgotten. Include the whole team in the process, giving everyone a chance to add something from themselves and think about what worked and what could be done better.

GETTING TOGETHER, REMOTELY

Even though we can now do more and more of our work individually and asynchronously, most projects will require a group gathering at some point. There are two ways to approach this: meetings and workshops. Meetings are more focused check-ins, while workshops are well-suited for creative brainstorming or problem-solving. Here, we'll review the best ways to approach meetings and workshops as a remote team..

REMOTE MEETINGS

Meetings are extremely important in remote collaboration. The fact that we all work from home or are physically separated from our co-workers means it's even more critical that we do them the right way to keep projects flowing and strengthen team bonds. When you're first switching to the remote or hybrid work model, it can be tempting to call them more often than you did in the office, as a substitute for in-person contact. But it's important to recognize that meetings need to be used and run differently than the ones you're used to in an office world.

You can have productive and engaging meetings even though you can't all physically congregate or pop into each others' offices. With virtual meeting tools, such as Zoom, Microsoft Teams, or Google Meet, you can organize real-time video conferences, while collaborating digitally in real-time with tools like Mural or Miro. There are really very few things that can't be done online – except maybe offering everyone coffee and cookies. Keep in mind virtual meetings come with a similar set of challenges as in-person meetings do. Though it might seem like meetings get in the way of productivity, with a remote team, they are necessary to keep everyone on track and updated.

Let's see what are the most popular types of meetings and how they should be organized.

	▼ What Are They?	▼ How to Run Them	▼ Tips & Tricks
Daily Stand-Up	A short, concise team status check, usually held at the same time each day. For example, it could be a 15-minute meeting to synchronize activities and create a plan for the next 24 hours.	Virtual stand-ups should last 10 to 20 minutes. Ask questions like "What did you get done yesterday (or last week, last month, etc.)?" and "What are you working on now?" or "Where do you need help?"	Only talk about things that are relevant to everyone involved. Write down any off-topic issues to address at another time.
One-on-One Meetings	Unlike structured stand-ups, status reports, and other types of meetings, one-on-ones are more flexible and allow for managers to give an employee their full attention and personalized feedback.	Ask questions like "What is stressing you out lately?" and "What would help you grow professionally or work more happily?" Invite the participant to tell you how you can better support them.	Mangers should ask their subordinates to help set the meeting agenda for 1:1 meeting Use it for complex and uncertain content, especially emotions, hopes, and fears.
Problem Solving Meetings	Teams use problem solving meetings to analyze a situation and its causes, assess what direction to take, then create an action plan to resolve the problem. They are perhaps the most complex and varied type of meetings. The hardest part can be agreeing on what the problem is in the first place!	Define the problem clearly and in as much detail as possible. (e.g. "Clients want to add a new feature to the app.") Then list your resources for solutions. (e.g. "We have 4 weeks of dev time and 5 people available to help.") Then brainstorm ways to solve the stated problem with the given resources and timelines.	Take notes somewhere visible, so participants see the information and progress. Make sure everyone on the team is involved and appoint a moderator to keep things on track. Always decide on next steps and assign action items before you finish the meeting.

179

MY OWN LESSONS IN REMOTE MEETINGS

Over the past three years, I've had over 1,500 virtual meetings, with thousands of people from around the globe. In the real world – during my travels or at conferences – I've met hundreds of new friends and acquaintances. You might think that relationships that are built mostly in the virtual space are cold or distant. No way! Even remotely, it's easy to build warm, meaningful relationships with new people – just be yourself!

For most of us, work meetings aren't very relaxed. Whether they're with colleagues or clients or business partners, we tend to be reluctant to behave in a completely natural way. It's a natural reaction, mainly related to the stress or pressure of such situations. And if that's the case in person, what happens when you move everything online, where you really have to demonstrate your participation rather than just being physically present? The very thought may make you feel slightly uncomfortable, even if you're extroverted.

Love meetings or hate them, but there's one thing we can all agree on: many of them are awful. In the United States alone, time wasted on inefficient, poorly conducted meetings costs companies $37 billion a year. According to an MIT study, managers who work with teams or projects throughout their careers spend 22 years (!) at meetings, seven of which are on meaningless conversations, meaningless presentations and office gossip.[37]

ELON MUSK advises his employees to "leave or log out of the meeting as soon as they feel that nothing is coming of it"[38].

So how can we improve meetings and reclaim that wasted time? Are so many meetings even necessary in the first place? Here, I'll guide you through some of the principles that keep me from spending half my life in ineffective meetings.

1 WHY ARE WE MEETING AT ALL?

Always ask yourself this question: *Should it be a meeting?* If there's another way to achieve the same outcome .... do it that other way! Never accept an invitation if it is not clear what the meeting's purpose is. Require the organizer to provide this information, minimum 24 hours before the meeting.

2 LONG LIVE AGENDAS!

If you've decided a meeting IS the best option, make sure it follows a well-established agenda – it is the key to success. Without it, it's easy to stray, the goal starts to blur, and time slowly but surely leaks through your fingers.

Start with proper preparation: find out in advance what participants want to talk about and what information they need to get out of it. Setting specific goals in advance isn't always easy, but it will help make sure every participant understands the objective of the meeting. It could be something as simple as "assign roles for the new finance project" or something broader, like "assess release strategy options for new product launch." Whatever it is, make sure everyone knows what the main topic is. Share the agenda with other participants no later than a day or two before the meeting, so that everyone has a chance to think about it and send any comments, as well as prepare their contributions.

Solid preparation is key to making the most of your time and avoiding – well, bullshit. Don't believe me? Then listen to Jeff Bezos: Yes, the billionaire founder of Amazon told his team to nix PowerPoints and start reading long pre-meeting memos in a "study hall"-like session before group gatherings.[39] Those meaty, meaningful memos help define scope in a way that long-winded slide presentations cannot, and help structure the narrative around what needs to be achieved. And, he has said,[40] it prevents busy or overburdened participants from trying to bluff their way through a meeting – a face-saving measure that helps no one in the long run. The process of writing and reading the memo can help keep the discussion on track and make it effective.

Jack Dorsey, Twitter CEO, also introduced the habit of reading an outline together before meetings, a process he summed up – how else? – in a tweet:.

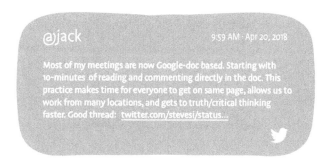

So if this practice works well in Amazon and Twitter, it will also work for your team.

If you want to really go crazy with the agenda, you can allocate a certain amount of time to each discussion point to encourage everyone to be brief and stay on topic. It's also worth prioritizing the agenda items, starting with the most important ones – this way, you're less likely to run out of time before you tackle the most important parts. Be realistic in your scheduling and make sure it's actually possible to get through the agenda in the allotted time; if you find you can't finish, make a note of it and take it into consideration when planning your next gathering.

3 CHANGE THE ATMOSPHERE

Start with an ice-breaker. For a Monday morning meeting, try asking: "How would you describe your weekend in one word?" And if you want to get people smiling, say, "Tell me which emoji suits you best today?" or "Which emoji best reflects your relationship to this project?" If you're talking about bringing your project to an international market, ask "what was your first-ever travel experience" or "what's the most interesting place you've ever visited?" It is important that the question is light, uncomplicated and allows for people to show a little personality. A little warm-up will set everyone at ease before you get to the serious work. Keep the tone going by making the meeting as interactive as possible – if the atmosphere is engaging, people won't feel left out or bored as you get through it.

4 DO VIDEO CALLS THE RIGHT WAY

- Discuss technical issues well in advance. If everyone knows which platform you are going to use, or whether you should have headphones at hand, you will save yourself the confusion and stress.
- A smile makes life easier! Use it to brighten up your co-workers' screens.
- Don't go overboard with sharing your screens. Let's be honest: PowerPoint slides are usually boring and no one really cares how much time you spend choosing fonts

5 A GOOD MODERATOR IS A GIFT

- At a larger meeting, identify someone in advance who will play the facilitator role, whether it's you or someone else. Someone needs to referee the time and organization of the conversation.
- If the conversation goes off the rails, don't be afraid to interrupt politely and bring everyone back to the main topic.
- When you've discussed everything you need to, bring the meeting

to a clear end; otherwise, the conversation will idle indefinitely.

- Use a timer if you really want to be efficient. You can make a game out of it to make it fun and save yourself and others from wasting precious minutes.

6 DON'T FORGET TO FOLLOW UP

- Make sure you agree on a plan for next steps. Everyone should log off with a clear vision of what you achieved and what action items they're responsible for completing.
- Check in with key players after for a post-mortem on how the meeting went and what else they might need.

REMOTE WORKSHOPS

Until now, workshops and brainstorming sessions have been associated with conference rooms and whiteboards covered in a million Post-It notes. Getting everyone in a room together was seen as the ideal way to handle conceptual work such as problem solving or introducing innovations. But is being locked inside four bland walls really the best way to collaborate? I've been in countless workshops where participants spent more time replying to e-mails than actively participating in the discussion. And I must admit: It wasn't always the participants' fault. Sometimes the leader was completely unprepared to conduct the event, or simply lacked the competence to do so.

Maybe, instead of worrying about being in the same physical space, we should be focused on the substantive issues? Stop insisting creativity comes from being in a room together and start taking a closer look how you prep and conduct the discussion. Workshops usually last longer and involve more people than your average meeting – and they're meant to deal with more important, strategic decisions. So once you break free of a conference room, what makes a workshop successful? Here are some advantages of switching to the virtual workshop mode:

1. **Document everything**

   Taking and sharing notes, organizing your thoughts, and making recordings of meetings are super easy when everything is online. It's effective as well and very convenient for participants!

2. **Save time**

   Digital tools save you a lot of time, both during and after the workshop. Want to recall what was said while discussing your marketing strategy for the next quarter? Search for a keyword in the transcript or scroll to the passage you need.

3. **Spend less**

   It's probably obvious: virtual workshops mean fewer expenses and less money spent on travel and organization.

4. **Move faster**

   Remote collaboration enables numerous, short attempts to solve a given problem. It encourages experimentation, which often leads to prototyping in or between meetings and helps you find the perfect solution faster.

5. **Increase participation**

   In real life, people with strong personalities can overwhelm the other participants ... which can negatively affect the outcome of your workshop. In the virtual format, everyone is on equal footing, which promotes openness and sharing your ideas. It's also possible for more people, or people from other cities or countries, to get involved.

6. **Save the planet**

   When you participate in a digital meeting, you leave the car at home and you don't buy a flight ticket. So your carbon footprint is minimal.

Of course, this doesn't mean organizing a remote workshop is easy. Technical issues can plague any online group activity, conversation can move slower or it can be harder to organize and monitor how engaged participants are, and you need to do more prep work to ensure everyone is one the same page once the event begins. However, if you really put your effort into it, you will be surprised how many new ideas can emerge and how much such collaborative work strengthens the spirit and creativity of the entire team.

In a virtual environment, you need to rethink how to run a workshop. Traditionally, in-person workshops mean getting the group together at one time, occasionally separating for smaller--group breakouts, and interacting with each other to build trust and creativity. A lot is changing in the remote world. For example, it's not necessary for everyone to be focused on the same task at the same time; instead, you might consider a combination of synchronous and asynchronous collaboration modes. Pre-meeting preparation or brainstorming can take place asynchronously, even before the participants see each other live. The remote environment might also affect how much work people do as a big group versus individually; it can be harder to break a big workshop group down into smaller conversational groups, simply because the tech issues become cumbersome. Technology can also limit non-verbal communication – when you're all sitting in front of the screens, it's harder to see positive or negative reactions from the group, to see when people are smiling or nodding along, or if they're eager to chime in and add to what the speaker is saying. At the same time, webcams, emojis, and other feedback in the digital world can sometimes be more honest or more affirming than the tougher-to--interpret in-person body language.

One thing is certain: remote workshops will look different than the in-person ones you are used to, but with proper preparation, planning and using the right tools, they can be even more productive. So let's see step by step how to go about it.

I. PLANNING THE WORKSHOP

Workshops rarely go smoothly on their own – usually they work best if they are prepared with a specific topic and audience in mind. The more effort you put into coordinating and organizing everything before you start, the better the results will be. Time spent preparing is time saved during the meeting. Plan carefully what you are meeting for, who will be present and how the workshop will run.

1 WHY ARE WE DOING THIS?

If anyone in your workshop asks the above question, you've failed in your prep work. Clarity of purpose is absolutely essential – none of the participants can have any doubts about it. Are you workshopping to align everyone toward a common goal or project? To build team trust? To solve a specific problem? To sprint on a design or functionality issue? Ask yourself:

- What is your main goal and expected result?
- Is the workshop the best means to achieve the goal?
- What information do participants need to have in order to join in effectively?
- How can you determine if the workshop was successful?

Once you have answered these questions, make sure that all workshop participants know them, too.

2 WHO WILL PARTICIPATE?

Check exactly how many participants there will be. Due to the lack of physical constraints, such as the size of a conference room, it might seem that the more the merrier. Nope! An easy way to stymie your workshop is to stuff it full of too many people. Not everyone needs to be there, and not everyone can actually contribute meaningfully. At the same time, you want to avoid having too few participants — if you don't have enough people to come up with fresh ideas, or to offer a diversity of knowledge and perspective, you won't come away with exciting results. Usually, the ideal number of participants should not be more than 20, although this obviously depends on the goal and composition. And remember: This isn't the only workshop that will ever happen — multiple rounds, or follow-ups with smaller groups, can help draw more from the experience.

Additionally, try to find out as much as possible about the participants: what do they do, what can they share with the rest, and what expertise might be lacking? How scattered are they around the world? Do they know each other well or not at all? You can't design the activities of the actual workshop without this information. Send surveys or do pre-workshop interviews if you need to.

3 SO ... WHAT WILL WE DO?

Plan the workshop carefully, select the best tools to conduct it, and think about ways to encourage people to actively participate.

3.1 TAKE CARE OF YOUR LOGISTICS

- Set a date and time. If the participants are scattered all over the world, this may not be easy. Take advantage of a time zone calculator such as World Time Buddy, or consider dividing the workshop into several sessions to enable active participation by people from the most extreme time zones. Take cultural differences into account: Will some participants have holidays or seasonal concerns, issues with meal times or necessary break times, or other responsibilities that will distract them from the workshop?

- Schedule the length of the workshop. An all-day experience is probably more than most effective workshops need. Most often, 2 to 4 hours is enough to warm up properly, have a meaningful meeting and summarize the results.

3.2 GET STARTED IN ADVANCE

- Send out detailed guidelines with the date and time of the meeting so that everyone knows when and how to participate.
- Start communication before the workshop. This could mean establishing a group chat or message board ahead of the workshop, or doing one-on-ones with people to prepare. Make sure everyone knows the goals, has the materials, and knows the rules before you begin.
- Prepare and share your agenda, notes, and other materials in advance so that everyone can study them carefully.
- Provide participants with basic etiquette rules, such as rules about when you should be on mute, arranging a quiet and focused workspace, making sure you're visible on screen and attentive when others are speaking, and not multitasking with other work while participating.
- Explain not only how you want the workshop to run, but also what will happen after it's over. Schedule a follow-up session to share reflections and information.

3.3 PLAN THE ACTIVITIES

- Choose what activities will be involved: brainstorming exercises, games, and any engagement methods that work for your goal and your group. Some activities might take more time, some less, but most should be under 30 minutes. Consider breaking down longer tasks into shorter sequences of one to five minutes to make them easier to digest.
- Try to create a flow to your workshop: If each activity is completely different, participants will end up feeling discombobulated or confused about where things are going. If you can create continuity for them by having activities that flow neatly from one to the next, you'll keep brains on the right track.
- Set an agenda. Estimate how long each task will take; set breaks; think how much time you can stand spending in front of a screen; and make sure each participant has enough time to speak.

3.4 CHOOSE THE RIGHT TOOLS

- Which video conferencing option is right for your workshop? Will you be a single group the whole time, or do you need something that allows for smaller group breakouts? Are the tools familiar enough for the participants to use without issue? Will any recorded materials be easy to distribute after the fact? Here's what you might need:
  - **Collaboration:** Well, you won't have a beautiful, shiny board and colorful markers, but digital whiteboards are just as useful – plus,

the space is infinite. With tools like MURAL or Miro, you can share ideas, illustrate concepts, track brainstorming, and work as a team in a creative way.

- **Video-conferencing:** Zoom, Microsoft Teams or Google Hangouts are the most popular solutions. Unless there is a real need, it's best to use them – most of the participants will know them well, which will save you from technical challenges and stresses. If your team is open to experimentation, you can try platforms such as Loop Team, RemoteHQ or Tandem, which combine video functions with collaboration applications.
- **Communication:** Messaging on Slack, Twist or Microsoft Teams can be useful. Google Docs, Confluence, Notion and Evernote are best for creating and storing informational text documents before and during the meeting.
- **Engagement:** Mentimeter, Stormz, Sli.do and other platforms will help you create and share interactive real-time polls, quizzes, surveys and Q&A options.

- Once you have decided which tools you will use, be sure to inform the participants well in advance. That way you can make sure everyone has the technical items they need to participate and you can provide any training or testing in advance for those who need extra help, without derailing the workshop itself. You could even try a test call before the main event, to ensure everyone can access and operate the tools they need. Do the tools work with every device or operating system? Are people prepared to switch fluidly between collaboration tools and video chat? Is the audio reliable? Is the experience visual enough to keep people engaged? Addressing these issues in advance will keep things on track. Establish a plan B in case a particular tool goes offline or technical issues crop up mid-workshop.

4 GET READY TO MODERATE

- Prepare talking points for yourself as the facilitator. You gotta have a plan at your fingertips, to make sure you know how things should flow and to ensure you don't miss anything in the chaos and collaboration of the moment. Setting a personal agenda for yourself – in addition to the public agenda you give participants – can help you make sure you have all the pieces in one place.
- Have a list of ways to deal with predictable situations, such as technology problems, participant conflicts, or stubborn walls of silence.
- Practice everything! It will seem silly, but acting out how things will go will help reveal any gaps in your planning.

II. CONDUCTING THE WORKSHOP

So you've prepped and communicated and everyone is ready to go … now is your moment of truth! Here are some tips for facilitating your workshop on the day of the event:

1 START STRONG

- Begin with a warm up. Ask everyone to briefly introduce themselves, especially if workshop participants represent different departments or different companies. Try icebreaker exercises or a get-to-know-each-other activity to kick things off, to reduce tension and build the rapport you need to have comfortable and creative discussions later. One of the more abstract icebreaker questions I've heard: "Which are better: Pirates or ninjas? And why?" These kinds of questions make for a very light introduction to a meeting.

- Be a good host! Lay out, quickly but clearly, what you'll do, what's expected of participants, and how to communicate. All logistical issues should be discussed at the very beginning.

- Remember that not everyone is comfortable with group video calls. So, if you feel an awkward tension and nervous silence at the very beginning, address the elephant in the room. Use humor to diffuse the discomfort of a new or uncertain situation. If you say what everyone is thinking, you'll be able to move past it sooner.

- Ask everyone to turn on their cameras (and don't forget to turn on your own). Participants should see each other so that nonverbal communication and engagement isn't lost, and so that there is a sense of familiarity among the participants.

- Set the right tone: One of the moderator's tasks is to create a friendly and positive atmosphere. Don't let technical problems, initial shyness and other small things break you out of the rhythm, and your good attitude will quickly spread to the other participants.

2 STAY ON TRACK

- **Keep up the pace:**

  Divide individual tasks into shorter segments, say 5-10 minutes, and use a timer to keep things on track. If you have to make a decision and are waiting for feedback from the team, a countdown is a good idea: "Five, four, three ... I can't hear any more ideas ... Two, one ... The decision has been made!"

- **Control the audio:**

  Ideally all of your participants have enough experience working remotely to know about mute buttons and hot mics, but you can never be sure. As the moderator, make sure any background noise isn't distracting or annoying. If the discussion is getting interrupted or off track, remind people of other tools — text chat, etc. — where they can communicate without needing to be audible to everyone.

- **Assign roles:**

  Determine who will moderate, who will lead the discussion, who will take notes, etc., to avoid randomness and chaos.

- **Maintain clarity:**

  Explain each exercise and what it should achieve. When an activity is finished, briefly review what happened and why.

- **Take breaks:**

  A well-prepared workshop will have break times scheduled to keep people fresh; however, as the moderator, you need to gauge everyone's energy levels and adapt accordingly. If everyone seems exhausted, or if an activity isn't working out, consider changing the plan.

- **Record everything:**
  Whether it's a video recording or another method, make sure there is a way for participants (and potentially others) to revisit the content later. Transcripts can help, especially if people want to search keywords or jump to certain points of the conversation.

3 KEEP PARTICIPANTS ENGAGED

- **Make people feel involved:**
  Pay attention to shy or quieter individuals; encourage them to take part in the discussion and make sure they do not get drowned out by louder or more enthusiastic participants. Kindly but firmly shut down interrupters, oversharers, or too-energetic participants, so that they don't annoy or intimidate the others. recall to be fair, people are too expressive and have a tendency to interrupt others.

- **Focus everyone's attention:**
  Keep people involved (and prevent them from multitasking with personal projects or other work) by doing spontaneous or spur of the moment queries — it could be polls, trivia, search results or anything that requires participants to drop what they are doing and respond quickly.

- **Get feedback frequently:**
  Ask for responses to the speaker's comments, input on how things are going, opinions on what to do next — anything that will get people to chime in.

- **Ask others to document:**
  Involve attendees in the recording process — taking notes, filling

in meeting materials, and other tasks as you go, to create materials that might be useful for archiving or sharing post-workshop.

- **Create a shared experience:**
Think of ways to connect people despite how widely scattered you all are. This could be a shared music playlist, or a running joke or repeated mantra that people will remember long after the workshop.

4 WIND THINGS DOWN

- **Do a final wrap-up:**
Don't let things end on a brainstorming note. Take time to summarize the most important discussion threads and overall goals at the end of the workshop
- **Make a to-do list:**
What should people plan to do as soon as the video call ends? If you have agreed on joint projects or tasks, assign them to specific people and make sure everyone is aware of their **responsibilities.**
- Ensure future communication:
Let people know how to contact you and each other later. Collect any notes or recordings made during the workshop and save them before everyone departs.
- **End on a positive note:**
No matter how the workshop goes, thank everyone for their participation and let them know their contributions are valued.

III. AFTER THE WORKSHOP: WHAT'S NEXT?

Congratulations, you have managed to bring the meeting to a happy end! Is that all there is? Not necessarily! Here's what to do next:

- **Document results:**

  Make a written summary of the meeting and its outcomes and send it to the participants. Include any key learnings, as well as next steps or tasks that came out of the brainstorming.

- **Share information:**

  Don't let a lot of good teamwork be wasted! Send out links to recordings, documents, transcripts, and anything else you might find useful. The data and discussion can prove useful to people who couldn't make the meeting, or to people at higher or lower levels who can use it to educate themselves on their own time.

- **Ask for feedback.**

  Encourage participants to give honest and constructive feedback about the workshop to find out what went well and what could be improved next time. Try e-mails, surveys, post-workshop polling or other mechanisms that let people share their thoughts. Some feedback may be best shared with the whole group; other feedback may be best one-on-one, or even delivered anonymously.

- **Keep the discussion going:**

  Create a messaging group, Slack channel or other community space, especially if the discussion was lively or you didn't have time to cover everything. Of course, moderating such channels is extra work, but if the good ideas are still flowing, it can be worth it!

- **Plan to reuse:**

  Can materials be turned into templates, or repurposed for future workshops?

FIRST-HAND

Spencer Waldron

As Head of Remote & Global Brand Communications Director at Prezi, Waldron is an expert in internal and external communication and understands storytelling can be the most effective tool for sales and marketing.

W We've seen in 2020 that many organisations and people survived the mass move to remote work by basically "copy / pasting" how they did things in the office, straight into the home. It was very clunky but somehow worked (because humans are amazing!) but after a few weeks and months the cracks started to appear.

I think that organisations started to realise that to "thrive", not just survive in a remote first setting there are a number of fundamental questions about culture that need to be asked.

One of those fundamental questions is – What is this meeting for?

Even before COVID, we all know that most people don't seem particularly happy with the results the meetings create. In a remote first setting the very essence of meeting culture needs to be challenged.

We tend to find, especially in large organizations, that lots of meetings are status updates, and status updates don't actually need to be a meeting. Now, sometimes, you might need to, but what we found, time and time again, is that instead of everybody sitting around for half an hour giving an update, people can literally record a two-minute video (if it's structured properly) to give their update, and then, people can watch it in their dedicated time for asynchronous communication.

It's also possible to reduce the length of meetings. The "jumping off information" that is given in a lot of meetings before discussion and decision-making happens can also be done asynchronously ahead of the meeting. Instead of someone talking for 15mins about the topic to set the stage so to speak, it can be structured properly and recorded as a 5min asynchronous video sent to people ahead of the meeting.

This has a lot of benefits. First people can watch the video at a time convenient to them. They can also watch it multiple times to soak in the information. They also have time to come up with intelligent questions, do any necessary preparation and come to the meeting ready for effective discussion and decision making.

Finally, it's entirely possible to remove meetings altogether. Asynchronous video can remove the need for you to be there sometimes when time zones don't match. For example, I was asked to come to a brainstorm meeting that was, for me, 9 o'clock on a Friday evening in Europe.

Now, first of all, I don't want to do a meeting at 9 o'clock on a Friday evening because … well it's Friday evening. But more than that I'm definitely not going to be creative.

So in my "deep work" time during the day, that's when I thought about it, brainstormed myself, did some research and then recorded a video with all of my ideas. I sent it to the team so they could play it in the meeting. Now sure, if possible, I'd always want to be present in a brainstorm as many ideas are built on top of each other. But this was a great solution and better than not contributing.

At the end of the day, you need to find and celebrate the people on your team who are doing things creatively — and encourage others to follow suit.

CHAPTER 9:

MANAGING REMOTELY

MORNING COFFEE: LISBON

Lisbon, September 2018. I'm ordering a double espresso as I watch the city come to life. Yesterday we ran the first workshop of Remote-how's experimental workation project. Three companies, more than 30 people, and one reflection – there is still a long way to go to better manage their daily tasks. So many people are still relying solely on e-mail exchanges and calendar updates when there are so many better tools and strategies out there for managing these tasks for remote teams. As I settle into the morning, I order my favorite local treat – a sweet pastel de nata. Thanks to a month of these indulgences, I'll leave Lisbon 7 pounds heavier than I arrived.

MY FIRST EXPERIENCES

As an inexperienced 22-year-old, thrown into the deep waters of managing a team in an international environment, I made a lot of mistakes. In retrospect, I see that those missteps stemmed from not knowing a lot of the basics that most managers learn from their superiors. I started out in an unusual way: I was reporting straight to the general director, who constantly traveled between Switzerland and Germany and the United States. From the very beginning, I realized how much depends on me – there was no one who was watching over my shoulder to check my work or give daily guidance. Instead, I had to be the one to take the initiative. In such circumstances, I quickly learned to be independent.

Now, with 10 years of work to look back on, I'm very glad that my career path was non-standard from the very beginning. I may have initially lacked some of the basics I'd have learned in a more traditional setting, but I got to be a meaningful player much earlier, and the mistakes I've seen along the way have inspired me to do everything I can to be a better leader – and to help others be the best leaders they can be.

Unfortunately, bad practices are common, and the pressure of targets and deadlines can often trump the desire to make changes to the way companies work. There is a serious lack of motivation and willingness to remodel management, especially at the highest levels of the corporate hierarchy. And changing attitudes is only half the battle – you still need to implement new solutions and root them firmly in the company's DNA.

If nothing else, 2020 forced even the most reluctant to confront this challenge. It was an opportunity to stop *talking* about changes and start *implementing* them. The age of office work is disappearing; so, too, should all the bad practices office culture has normalized over the years. But it won't happen automatically – it's up to managers (and employees) to put in the effort it takes to shift company culture to a healthier, more productive style that fits our new remote age.

CHANGE YOUR APPROACH TO MANAGEMENT

First things first: Leadership isn't easy. As remote work spreads, managers have to adapt to the new realities of motivating teams across both time zones and the barriers of old bad habits.

Selecting the right people for management positions has always been a challenge. Gallup's research shows that only about 10% of us have a natural predisposition to lead others.[41] This means that many people in managerial positions don't have the necessary skills, and in 82% of cases, companies choose the wrong managers. [42]

The wall full of degrees and trophies doesn't do much to establish your leadership cred in a virtual world. Instead, remote and hybrid teams need leaders whose authority and expertise are evident in their actions and achievements. They also need to be solid planners – charm and spontaneity can't run the day when your team is scattered across 10 locations in four time zones. In this new world, leadership isn't about looking like the strongest person in the room – it's about the relationships you can foster and the people you can motivate to work independently.

There are many factors to consider when handling distributed teams. With limited verbal communication and sometimes nonexistent physical interaction, managers can struggle to feel like they're influencing their team in the right direction. But leadership in an increasingly virtual environment is just leadership with a slightly different look and feel. Here are ways to adapt your leadership instincts to a remote team or company:

1 BECOME A MENTOR

Brian Knopp, director of human resources at Gartner, told The Wall Street Journal that managers of the future will need skills that are "less technical and more socio-emotional to help employees find in the culture of the organization."[43] And according to

Harvard Business Review, the best managers need to look to the field of coaching – and all the ideas about motivation and professional development that come from that arena – to truly know how to move their teams forward.

How to be a mentor to your team? There are countless books and tutorials on this, but as a quick overview, here are some ideas:

- Go beyond the results of the current project.

  Get interested in the long-term aspirations of employees, and try to get to know – to a reasonable extent – their interests and private life. Rather than just checking up on current assignments, ask more general, open-ended questions about what they really want to achieve.

- Stay optimistic.

  It's not just about smiling, although that also helps. Since you're going to support the employees in achieving their long-term goals, you must avoid attitudes like "I can't", "I don't have time" or "I can't", which are often the cause of professional frustration. Instead of stacking up obstacles, suggest solutions and ask more general questions to understand how you can help your subordinates achieve their goals. Encourage sharing opinions and voicing your own opinion, to make them feel you are taking care of them.

- Require responsibility.

  Think about it: At the gym, a good physical trainer develops a program for his client with detailed goals, deadlines, and workout and dietary requirements to help him achieve the results he wants ... and then scrupulously checks that the training goals are being achieved. A good manager of a distributed team does the same: he helps employees chart a path to their goal and then regularly checks that they are following it. You have to make so that your team feels responsible for the effects of their own work.

2 TRUST FROM A DISTANCE

Your team might not always be able to see you, walk into your office for a chat .... but if you give them reason to think you're telling them the honest, unvarnished truth about the work and your role in it, you can garner loyalty, support and productivity, even when you're dispersed remotely. On the trapeze of remote work, where we're always flying a little bit blind, you need to be sure that your manager will guide you and support you. Do whatever you can to build and strengthen relationships with team members. Let everyone know how important transparency and openness are in your cooperation.

In the preceding chapter, I talked about how social interaction can have an impact on collaborative team output. Mostly, I was focusing on the need for casual social connection; but teams also need leaders who will build their connections in more structured, dynamic ways. Back in the day, retreats and team-building exercises like "trust falls" — wherein the participants learn to let go, fall backward, and trust that the other members of their team will catch them — could help build a sense of unity and reliability. The pandemic era of as-little-touching-as-possible means those sorts of games and face-to-face learning and growth opportunities are fairly limited right now; but as The Wall Street Journal has highlighted, the off-site retreat is in need of a comeback (and possibly a makeover) as a means of keeping distributed teams connected.[44]

When we are able to meet again without masks and the constant disinfection of hands, the trips will be a great opportunity to get to know each other beyond our laptop screens, and to establish more direct and personal relationships. GitLab regularly organizes meetings of the entire company (around 1,300 people!) in various places around the world, and one of the employees describes them as casual meetings rather than typical conferences.[45]

The scope of these sort of in-person gatherings (should they include everyone? Be team-specific?) will depend on your company and team needs. So will what happens at the event itself. At Automattic, an all-company intensive might entail a 14-hour (or longer day) of flash talks that highlight people's interests and ice-breakers; collaborative work-related projects and non-work-oriented social activities and learning experiences; meals that aim to mix up who you're talking to; and even group runs and other get-to-know-everyone efforts.[46] At Buffer's (pre-pandemic) week-long 2017 retreat, 75 people came together in Madrid and followed an elaborate schedule mixed required professional conversations with optional fitness, arts and skill-sharing activities, with some free time thrown in for good measure.[47] This mindful approach took note of the needs of introverts and extroverts, and ways to blend career--building and company-specific work with the sort of low-key, fun social time that people need to truly bond. But simpler retreats — even just an afternoon together — can go a long way in solidifying the trust you, as a leader, need to build among your team members.

3 RETHINK HOW YOU RATE ACHIEVEMENTS AND PROGRESS

Ladies and gentlemen, in 2021, micro-management should definitely be a thing of the past. In the new world, the key is to give your team the freedom and independence to do their best work, while fostering their faith that you have their backs. The old way was casting an eye over the office to see who was at their desks. It can be tempting to apply this mentality to remote work, even when you can't see the staff: *Have they gone idle on chat? Is their camera off in meetings?* Resist this urge! A pillar of remote work is that individuals can work in different ways and locations toward the same goal. So let them!

This means shifting the understanding of "are you working?" from "are you physically in front of your computer?" to "is the work actually getting done?" Turn the focus to accomplishments, and use those as the goal posts for evaluating who is pulling their weight and earning their share. If the tasks are carried out and the team is satisfied, then so should the manager, shouldn't it?

4 PROACTIVE COMMUNICATION

We have repeated many times that in the remote world, good communication is the key. Keeping in touch and on top of communication is critical in a virtual environment. It's how you keep projects moving forward, keep workers productive, and keep the team from feeling too far away. Make an effort to initiate contact as often as possible and to embrace clarity as a driving principle in how you communicate with your team. Creating streams of feedback can both give information to your employees and help you get information about their successes and challenges out of them. Daily stand-ups via video conferencing can help with this. So can regular "how are you feeling?" temperature checks – when you're not going to catch someone having an off day in the break room, you need other ways to test their highs and lows and keep them on track. Try to avoid communication lapses that let employees "fill in the blanks" on their own – meaning, with their own concerns, fears, paranoia or worries.

TEAM COMMUNICATION AUDIT

A good way to assess the effectiveness of communication with employees is to audit your own habits in this area. How to do it? Here are the next steps:

- **BEFORE THE AUDIT**
  Review your activities from the last two weeks. You can look in the mailbox, call log, SMS and corporate chat to recall the details, although it is not absolute precision that is the purpose of this task.
  - **PQuestion 1.** How often have you communicated with: 1) your manager; 2) your immediate supervisor (and in what form)? Count and enter the results in the appropriate fields.
  - **Question 2.** How often did they communicate with you (and in what form)? Count and enter the results in the appropriate fields.
  - **Question 3.** How do you rate the frequency of communication with individuals (just right, too much, too little)?

- **Question 4.** How do you rate the quality of communication? Were the messages clear and set in the right context?
- AFTER THE AUDIT

1. Enter the communication rules

- **Frequency:** What is the optimal and desired level?
- **Tools:** What form of communication works best in a given relationship?
- **Speed:** How long do you expect responses to different types of messages (urgent, for news, progress report, request for feedback)?
- **Content:** What information does the person expect (only the most important, detailed, only progress, problems only etc.)?

2. Establish accessibility standards

- How often will we have formal meetings?
- Can we arrange regular appointments one for one every week, with the possibility of postponing them from time to time?
- What degree of insight into each other's calendars should we allow each other?
- At what times can you connect with people in other time zones and reply to their messages?
- Does your manager intend to introduce fixed working hours for the team?

5 FORMULATE CLEAR EXPECTATIONS

If everyone on your team can't start their day knowing exactly what you're expecting from them ... you've dropped the ball. Because

Quality

KIND OF COMMUNICATION AND CONTEXT (high / medium / low)

Quantity

JUST ENOUGH?
TOO LITTLE?
TOO MUCH?

OTHER TYPES OF COMMUNICATIO

PERSONALLY

PHONE CALLS

TEXT MESSAGES

VIDEO MEETINGS

E-MAIL

My manager

My project lead (if applicable)

Another supervisor (if applicable)

My manager

My project lead (if applicable)

Another supervisor (if applicable)

My communication with ....

Communication with me ....

you're working outside of face-to-face check-ins, people need to be able to move forward or go heads-down on a project with confidence that they are on track and doing the right thing.

Make sure the team knows the expectations by giving them specific examples, creating clear workflows and tools like task calendars, and utilizing frequent proactive communication. It can also help to have a clear routine – a mental muscle memory of how things need to work – to help people frame their time and tasks. And establishing a finish line – final deadlines and a clear vision of what you'll have achieved by the end – can help add clarity to what needs to go on.

6 MOTIVATION MATTERS

There's always a reason we show up to work in the morning (or afternoon .... or evening ...) Sure, the salary is a primary motivator. But there are plenty of other reasons to put in the time and effort at work. And keeping those motivations high is a key role of any leader.

Physical separation can create a tricky disconnect, and people can easily interpret silence as being ignored. You need to keep them engaged. You want to be able to bring out the best in your team – their top-level creativity, their strongest productivity, and their most fluid ways of working together.

Figure out what motivates your team by digging in via one on one breaks from the daily grind and introspective questioning. Getting to know your team will help you understand what's driving each person; in turn, that helps you keep each individual – and the entire project – on track.

Find ways that help your team collaborate despite the physical distance. Make sure there is clarity on what the company stands for, what its mission is, and why the work matters; a sense of camaraderie and unity can help people understand why they and their work matter. Try encouraging team members to reach out to you – and to their fellow colleagues – about positive things, like birthdays, or asking for advice, or offering congratulations. If every interaction isn't a chore or a negative connection, people will feel more inspired to work together. Team building activities can help with this – happy hours, hobby meet-ups, and other virtual events can keep people connected.

At the end of the day, you want people to be independently motivated to do their best work; listen when they tell you how to do that.

7 EMPATHY ABOVE ALL

Especially in the post-2020 age, a little bit of understanding about difficult times and circumstances can make all the difference in creating a harmonious workplace. Empathy is the ability to share or understand the feelings of others – and boy, it has never been more necessary than now. A Businessolver report even suggests that as much as 60 percent of remote workers would take a pay cut if it meant working in a more empathetic environment.[48]

From a practical point of view, empathy often boils down to just .... listening. Hear what your team is saying, find out what they are worried about, what's causing them stress or anxiety. Repeating back what people say, letting them know you hear and value their input, can help grow that trust. Keep tabs on who is more engaged and who is more isolated, and try to find out why. Ask them how they are navigating the hard parts of remote life – the isolation, or the cramped space, or the unfettered freedom. Pay attention to your surroundings and the people in them – even virtually – to make sure that your decisions about your team are guided by empathy.

8 NIP CONFLICTS IN THE BUD

So it's finally happened – you've hit a snag. One of your team members is unhappy, or butting heads with another; a project is off track and everyone is pointing fingers at someone else for the blame. Conflict is inevitable, even in the smoothest-running workplace, and especially with the communication deficiencies that remote work must overcome. So being prepared for how to manage it remotely will keep small problems from becoming big hurdles.

> The worst thing you can do is ... do nothing and expect things to work out all on their own.

Sure, it can seem easier to brush things under the rug, or wave them off as small issues that people will "get over." But that almost always ends up being a recipe for disaster, as animosity or uncertainty festers into an unhappy daily work life. Instead, address things head on – the sooner, the better.

The other thing to avoid is assumptions. Go into any conflict mediation with as much information as possible. From there, ask questions from a place of curiosity and fact-finding: the answers will provide you with some data about what's going on, but it will also give you insight into how the conflicting parties are feeling about it. Keep an eye on yourself to make sure you're really listening to what's being said and not assuming anything based on past experiences or your initial impressions of the issue. And keep an eye on the people involved to consider whether there is more going on beneath the surface – is this conflict really about the project deadline, or who carried more of the task burden? Or is it stemming from a bigger or quieter source of frustration?

Keep the dialogue neutral and revealing with questions such as:

- Can you help me understand what happened?
- Can you give an example?
- What was the effect of this behavior?

And keep your listening active – give the participants a chance to hear how they're being interpreted, and allow them to course correct or confirm as needed, by saying things like:

- I want to make sure that I understand you well ...
- From what I understand you are saying that ...
- Did I get that right?

In the end, make sure to follow up with participants one on one and make sure whatever solution you agreed to is being followed through.

TIME FOR RADICAL CANDOR

There are a number of ways to adjust your management style or company culture to better function in a remote environment, but one of the ways of gaining traction involves being as brutally honest as possible.

The concept of "radical candor" can make a major difference in a remote environment, but it can be jarring for some workplaces to adopt. Author and CEO coach Kim Scott explains that "radical candor" means giving feedback directly and without cushioning — even in a way that might be perceived as harsh or critical by modern professional standards. In her time at Google, she once said, Sheryl Sandberg pulled her aside after a meeting and gently pointed out that she said "um" a lot. The meeting had otherwise been a success, so Scott says she kept brushing off the "um" critique, until Sandberg bluntly told her:

"You know, Kim, I can tell I'm not really getting through to you. I'm going to have to be clearer here. When you say um every third word, it makes you sound stupid.'" Scott admits that without that bluntness, she wouldn't have paid attention to the problem and fixed it.[49]

On a chart delineating how much you care personally and how much you might challenge someone, radical candor is what happens in the top-right quadrant:

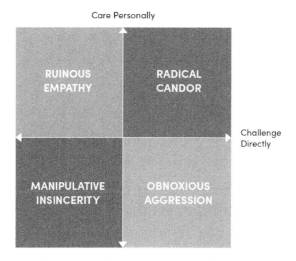

It's about worrying less about what's polite and appropriate, and saying what you mean with a heavy dose of concern for the other party's well-being. If you never criticize something that's going wrong or challenge the way someone is holding things back, you're also not providing people the opportunity they need to make a correction or improve. And that feels more unfair than facing a blunt criticism.

In an office, criticism can be delivered with some of the in-person social nuances that take the edge off — tone of voice, interpersonal relationships, facial expressions, and time can all come into play. Offices are naturally prone to limiting direct challenges and blunt criticism, because the face-to-face closeness can make getting over that potentially negative experience more difficult. But remote work requires a different way of interacting, and in an asynchronous and socially limited environment, an openness and acceptance of radical candor can help fast-forward through conflict and drama to the heart of a problem.

It's not about being rude or mean, but about shedding some of the social niceties that weigh down conflict resolution; if your team has a strong foundation of trust and respect, it will make it easier to accept the truth or challenge without hurt feelings or sensitivities. Radical candor can also help prevent backstabbing among teammates and save managers from wasting time with back-and-forth diplomacy about who said what about whom; if nothing else, it's going to be efficient!

But in all seriousness, it can also be an important cultural touchstone that allows people to speak truth to power— which in some cases, as a manager, is going to mean you. As much as you need to encourage your employees to be direct and challenging when necessary with each other, you, too, need to be braced for honest feedback. Find ways to allow your team to approach you with their own radical candor moments.

UNIFY YOUR TEAM

As a manager, you have a responsibility to ensure that your team is unified, that its members trust you and each other, and want to work together. Team-building exercises will help you achieve this goal. Here are some of the most interesting methods we've gathered in Remote-how:

- **Road to target**

  Encourage everyone to share their chosen goals with others. Let everyone introduce one – it can be joking or quite serious, related to work or private life. By sharing them with the whole group, everyone cares more about their implementation and achievement. How to do it? It's easy!

  - Plan a meeting and advise everyone about the idea for everyone had time to devise and prepare his own goal for discussion.
  - We start with managers! Tell me about the task you set yourself to encourage others to be open by your example.
  - When you are done, ask team members to share their goals one by one and how they intend to achieve them.
  - Document everything. You can enter your goals in the team calendar or put them in another public document. Remember to set deadlines!
  - Check your implementation regularly and share your impressions.

  Talking about your goals in a forum and putting them on a shared calendar can be very motivating for you to put in effort to really achieve them. Even if not everyone succeeds, cheering each other on for sure will make you stronger as a team.

- **Who is this?**

  This exercise will help you get to know your co-workers better – and make you surprised more than once!

  - Ask everyone to bring back photos of themselves from the past or they thought about something that that nobody on the team knows about. Then have everyone pass on their "secrets" to the facilitator – it can be you, as the team manager, or some other person of your choice.

- The leader of the game displays photos or information provided by friends as slides, and the rest tries to guess who they are talking about.

The game is very simple, but it is always accompanied by a lot of laughter, it is also conducive to bonding and getting to know each other better. The more so that often the ambition of each participant turns out to be to come up with something about himself that others will surely, but certainly not guess!

- **Interactive meeting**

Slido, which created the platform for engaging the public during offline and online lectures, uses live polls among employees during its monthly internal meetings to involve everyone in the meeting – including people present remotely. One way is to play the silent hero. Each team member nominates a different person who, in their opinion, deserves recognition for their work unnoticed by the general public. As the process progresses, the names start appearing on the screens in the form of a cloud. CEO Peter Komornik also used real-time surveys to present data on the company's condition – he asked, for example, a multiple-choice question about the results for last quarter. Interactive quizzes can, in turn, introduce an element of competition to team meetings and help both assimilate information and strengthen bonds.

- **Show and tell ...**
  Prezi holds "Show 'n Tells" every other week to bring its international offices together for company updates, product launches, and more. People dial in from each location and take turns presenting information about what they've been working on – sometimes marking special achievements with pre-coordinated cake and champagne.

Of course, these are just a few ideas for integrating games. Anything that allows you to laugh, talk and spend time together will definitely have a positive effect on the team spirit and productivity.

MANAGEMENT IN A MULTICULTURAL ENVIRONMENT

International, multicultural, global, borderless – whatever term we choose, the fact is that dispersed teams are becoming more and more diverse. This is great news, of course. Remote work allows you to draw on a larger pool of talents from around the world, it also increases the range of perspectives, points of view and experiences present in the company.

> Research shows that multicultural teams adapt faster to changes in the business environment.[50]

But with diverse hiring comes a whole host of new issues in creating a unified team culture. When your workforce hails from around the globe, it can raise issues of language barriers or cultural norms. Differing employee lifestyles can also be a hurdle: Meshing a work-from-home parent of three kids with a digital nomad kite surfer can lead to culture class or misunderstandings about expectations and ways of operating.

Certainly there are pitfalls. Communication can break down as a result of language barriers. There can be cultural information gaps – information or idioms or ways of doing business that are "a given" in one part of the world might not be so obvious to team members who grew up in a different part of the world. Cultural norms around workplace behavior and expectations, and the role of leadership, can create tension for the unprepared. But with solid and consistent leadership, even the most divergent of teams can come together as a healthy, functional and respectful unit.

So how do you make everyone feel comfortable and safe? A separate book could be written about it! Below I will focus on a few of the most important matters.

1 FIND WAYS TO MAKE DIVERSITY ADVANTAGE

Even if everyday collaboration in a multicultural team sometimes leads to tensions and misunderstandings, try to highlight how this diversity improves and improves your work – both on an individual and group level. Admitting openly that you are different, rather than pretending that you are all the same, will foster an atmosphere of honesty and transparency. Having a baseline understanding that the differences are a good thing sets a strong foundation for resolving issues.

2 KEEP LEARNING AND ADAPTING

The process of becoming sensitive to cultural differences is ongoing and evolving – it's not an end point, it's a journey. This can be as basic as making sure team members know what time zones their counterparts in other parts of the world are really in, to knowing background about their country, local holidays, major news that may be impacting them, and other touchstone data that can help people feel known. On the flip side, this can also mean correcting your team when they make mistakes, such as relying on stereotypes or making inappropriate comments, assumptions or jokes.

3 WORDS MATTER

Even when everyone on the team speaks a single language, it's important to remember that the degrees of fluency may vary more than you think. Different vocabularies, accents, and cultural knowledge may impact the way you're being heard and also what you're hearing from the team. For this reason, it can help to speak slowly and with good, clean grammar. I know that sounds obvious, but the way we talk in everyday life is not always textbook-level, and meandering around through confusing linguistic mistakes can throw off non-native speakers. Avoid using filler words (um, or like) and pare back on the slang, idioms and fancy vocabulary words until you have a better sense of how much your team really understands. It's not about dumbing anything down; it's about keeping things as straightforward as possible to avoid possible confusion or offense.

4 LISTEN ACTIVELY

Active listening can help ease communication issues with any remote team, but it can especially smooth over cross-cultural communication wrinkles. It involves shifting from a version of listening in which you silently absorb what the speaker is saying, to a version that is engaged and requires some back-and-forth. You can try to repeat back what someone has said, to be sure you've understood them correctly.

- "So, if I'm understanding, you mean ...."
- "So what you're saying is ..."

In addition to rephrasing to ensure comprehension, ask a lot of questions – even, occasionally, if you know (or think you know) the answer. This can help build the speakers confidence as an authority on a subject, or give them a chance to add detail they might otherwise have missed. It also shows that you're engaged and connecting with what they are saying. Make sure the questions are more than closed yes/no questions.

You can also try writing things down – either during conversation, to make sure you're understanding, or as an after-conversation follow-up, to give them a chance to follow up or correct any problems. (Sometimes, written language abilities can be stronger than off-the-cuff speaking abilities.) Active listening can build rapport and decrease the chance of misunderstandings or missed information.

5 REMEMBER: WE'RE ALL HUMAN

Never lose sight of your workforce as individual people who need help. When someone is struggling, find ways to pull them back into synch with the rest of the team. Provide the flexible arrangements that will make everyone comfortable, regardless of their location, background, family or personal needs, or cultural routines. When there is conflict, address it head on, and immediately, to avoid letting misunderstandings fester and bad feelings draw cultural dividing lines among colleagues. Finally, find ways to foster those human connections between the members of your team, so that their growth is a source of bonding.

IS YOUR PROJECT MANAGEMENT STRATEGY WORKING?

Keeping projects on task is critical to keeping your remote company afloat in difficult times like a pandemic — it's the junction of efficiency and productivity. But if you're not managing the projects appropriately, you can lose as much as 10 percent of every dollar you're pulling in. At Remote-how, in conjunction with Toggl, we developed frameworks to assess how your remote team is handling project management.[51] Using these frameworks for a project management audit means evaluating the project goals, who's in charge of managing it, which team members need to contribute or participate, to discover any weak spots and provide solutions on how to patch them. The goal is to figure out if the project management system you're using fits your overall needs and expectations, helping your project meet any regulatory, legal or financial compliance standards, make sure the scope and budget for your project are realistic, that work is shared evenly amongst the participants, and that any potential risk is identified and addressed as early in the project as possible.

HOW TO DO A PROJECT MANAGEMENT AUDIT

1 PLAN

Make a list of project participants to be interviewed or consulted — from full-time employees and project leads down to freelancers or minor assisting contributors. Write down the questions you intend to ask them. You want to get consistent and complete information from each interview the first time, with no gaps. You'll also need to plan ahead to make sure you've gathered all of the documentation and data you need. Is there a contract, statement of work, written guidelines of any kind that are being used to guide the project? Does your organization have particular quality control mechanisms or guidance? Look for any documentation that's already been established and identify any that's missing. Remember that the planning phase isn't just about going along with whatever the documentation says, it's also about challenging what isn't there and needs to be.

2 LEARN

Interview project participants one on one, asking them about their current role and the scope of their involvement with the project. Pay attention to all of the different viewpoints that crop up as you talk to different people. Approach it as an information--gathering exercise, rather than a critical one, or an attempt to find fault. Make sure the people you interview know that your end goal is to help make their work easier, not to assign blame. At the same time, review the project documentation you collected in the planning phase and determine: Is it being updated regularly and accurately? Is it a clear assessment of where the project stands? Which pieces are missing?

3 REVIEW

Now comes the most important part — taking the mess of interview information, project documentation and planning materials, and assessing where things really stand. Make a list of the challenges that you identified during your interviews with the project participants and compare them with documents and records to see if everything lines up – and if not, figure out where the discrepancies are. They can be:

- **Planning errors:** Does the project have a clear timeline and a system in place for documenting progress along that timeline? If not, establish a clear statement of work and linear approach to achieving it.
- **Management errors:** Do employees have trouble finishing tasks within the set deadlines? Do they have difficulty identifying who is responsible for what tasks? If so, try to be precise as to who should be carrying out specific tasks.
- **Workload errors:** Are people taxed to their limits and feeling frustrated? Or is work coming in at a lower standard than you would expect or desire? It's possible people are being overworked or that expectations are too high. Redistributing work, or using new tools to track progress, can help.
- **Tool errors:** Your choice of online or software tools to track performance and progress matters even more in a remote environment. If the ones you are using are clunky or inefficient, cumbersome to manage or confusing, you may need to switch to new ones or provide better training so that they become less burdensome and more effective. The right tools should minimize errors, not increase them.

4 EVALUATION AND RECOMMENDATIONS

Collect all findings, compare them with the audit objectives and criteria, and see if the project management process you're using has passed or failed the test. Above all, however, make recommendations for improvement and suggest how to implement them.

LET'S GET TO WORK!

Virtual project management is not easy, especially if your company was forced to switch to this mode of operation unexpectedly. It can feel like you are a little lost at sea as you try to navigate through new processes and procedures. Just remember that everyone on the team is feeling the same way. So take the bull by the horns: You can achieve your project goals working remotely; it will just require a shift in the way everyone thinks and works.

FIRST-HAND

Darren Murph

Currently the Head of Remote at GitLab and hailed by CNBC as an "oracle of remote work", Murph has led and mentored many remote teams and earned a Guinness World Records spot as the most prolific and most cited blogger.

The smartest, most transparent, and most progressive companies transitioning to remote will hire an executive to lead their journey in the next one to two years. This hire (or the lack thereof) will be a litmus test to job seekers who expect remote work to be supported, not merely allowed.

The difference is immense. My wife and I adopted a newborn at birth, growing our family through a beautiful, open relationship with our son's birth mother. Being supported as a remoter meant zero judgment when I took midday breaks to handle meetings necessary to move an adoption forward. Support was giving me the tools and psychological safety to work in a non-linear fashion, and I feel the difference each time I look at our son.

A Head of Remote ensures that onboarding, learning and development, and existing workflow evolution enables a company's culture and business to thrive regardless of where any one person sits on a given day.

Given enough time, the concept of remote as a precursive descriptor for work will become superfluous. Thus, it's vital to hire not only a change agent for today, but a visionary for the future. The natural evolution of the Head of Remote role is a chief strategist to oversee all workplace experience.

Transitioning to remote work is not a binary switch that is flipped. Remote is a journey of iteration — a tireless, evolving trek that demands a senior visionary and leader, or else your firm risks falling back into conventional habits or creating a fractured culture where no one is clear on what is expected.

Existing executives do not have space to carve out a third or more of their time to solve these issues. Moreover, these challenges are not one-and-done. Diversity and inclusion isn't a one-time problem to solve; neither is real estate strategy, or pricing, or endpoint management, or benefits realignment.

Prior to the COVID-19 pandemic, remote was predominately viewed as a career killer. Due to geographic biases and a stubborn resistance from traditional organizations to embrace more fluid and inclusive ways of working, there is now an acute shortage of tenured, senior-level remote strategists.

The most important quality in a remote leader is experience: there is no substitute for years. From there, it's a nexus of vision, compelling storytelling to influence buy-in, the ability to drive or partner with operational change agents, and a comfortability advising executives, investors, and stakeholders globally. Where this role sits depends on the organization — it's suitable in marketing, design, finance, and people. Many firms may indeed need a team, not just an individual, depending on the scale of the transformation and existing remote fluency.

The larger your organization is, or the more deeply it is entrenched in co-located tradition, the more significant the challenge and compensation expectations. This role will be far more complex in a hybrid-remote setting compared to an all-remote setting, as you're answering every question twice.

CHAPTER 10:

BURNOUT

MORNING COFFEE: HỘI AN, VIETNAM

It's almost 2 p.m. and this is only my first coffee of the day. I'm still recovering from a rough night, during which I hardly slept. Sometime around 2 a.m., I woke up in a brutal sweat with a fever of 102 degrees. Ola brought me one cold compress after another, but nothing would bring my temperature down. Did I need another round of fever meds? Should we call a doctor? What if it was actually COVID? No, it couldn't be, not here in Vietnam in February 2021, when the country has contained all active cases and we are – knock on wood! – rather safe. We came to the conclusion that there could be only one cause: I've been working too much. It's not the first time overwork has led to physical consequences. And now, after a grueling couple of months with extra projects and intense deadlines, my body has gone on strike. It's as though my body is saying "Iwo, slow down, you're working too much! I can't go at full speed from 6:30 a.m. to 10 p.m. every day! You have to change something!". My workaholic nature is getting the best of me.

LET'S TALK ABOUT HEALTH

Unfortunately, even in this day and age, mental health remains a taboo subject. We're not as open about things like depression or anxiety as we are talking about physical problems. There's still a stigma around mental health problems; as a result, people who suffer from them often have to face the challenge on their own.

And yet, mental health problems are among the diseases most threatening to our society. Our attitudes about work aren't helping – long hours and prolonged periods of high stress can cause problems or make them worse. The coronavirus pandemic is exacerbating the issues for many people – days, weeks, and months spent stuck at home have left a heavy mark on our psyche.

How can we help each other if we still can't talk openly about our mental health? Fortunately, there's a chance to change this, and our new way of working can help – as long as we really take care of openness and transparency in it.

WARNING SIGNS

Ten years – it took me so long to realize that work was not everything. The first of several "awakening" moments came in January 2019. Remote-how had been in operation for over a year: We'd landed our first clients, built exciting relationships with international partners, and received our first round of financial investment – nearly $400,000 – before we even had a tangible product to offer. Things were going great!

But getting to that point had been grueling. For the previous five years, I'd been pushing myself harder and harder through never-ending workdays, keeping up with a full-time job while getting my entrepreneurial dreams off the ground, powering through high-stress deadlines and all the pressure I could pile on myself. And then, it happened: After a marathon of almost non-stop work, my body gave out. Suddenly, I was consumed by a skyrocketing fever; for 48 hours, I could barely move from bed, let alone work. I convinced myself it was a fluke – I just have to power through! It was a crucial time for Remote-how. I couldn't afford to take time off when we were expanding the team and making major decisions. So on the third day, I rolled up my sleeves and got back to the grind.

Unfortunately, we soon hit a rough patch. Like any young entrepreneur, I made a few mistakes along the way and some of our ambitious plans didn't work out the way we wanted. We soon hit a financial wall. By the fall of 2019, we had to start drastically reducing expenses and the threat of bankruptcy was looming. I feared it could spell the end of our big dreams to change the world via remote work. The responsibility for bringing in the revenue we needed fell to me and my sales deputy, who revamped the sales department and became my backbone. We gambled everything on a new offering: A dynamic education program for managers of remote teams. It ended up being a bull's eye – in four months we had over 200 clients!

Our hard work had paid off, but it cost the entire team an enormous amount of stress. We all needed a reset, a complete break from work ... but suddenly that became impossible. Soon after we hit our client target, the pandemic took hold and the whole world was rapidly transitioning to remote work. Resting was NOT an option. Somehow I kept up the pace, until April, when another bout of brutal exhaustion hit me. It was preceded by typical signs of burnout: fatigue, lack of energy, and succumbing to unhealthy habits, such as skipping meals and avoiding exercise. I was working non-stop, if not always very effectively.

Then, in February 2021, I suffered my third physical breakdown – the one I mentioned at the beginning of this chapter. I knew this had to be the last time I let myself burn out so completely. I decided (and was rightly forced by my worried wife) to only allow early-morning or late-night meetings on my calendar two days a week. I started using Headspace, a meditation app, to keep my mind clear. And I committed to going work-free on weekends to give me a much needed release. It's just the beginning, and we'll have to wait and see if it's enough.

WAKE UP FROM THE AMERICAN DREAM

After all of this, I wondered how and why I found myself in such a place. How could I forget that life is not about working 10 or 12 hours a day, even if I love and enjoy it? That it is also worth doing other things: cultivating a hobby, helping others, investing in self-development, or just relaxing? Our society has long been guided by the ideal of hard work; but over time, it turned into a glorification of the hustle over everything else. I might be a Polish guy, but the idea of the "American dream" – that with enough hard work and initiative, you can climb to the top and achieve your wildest dreams – doesn't stop at the U.S. border. That dream has spread over the whole world, and I bought into it entirely. I rushed into projects, took huge risks, and functioned in a state of permanent stress. If I wasn't trying to do everything, then I wasn't doing enough, was I?

It's an all-too-common mentality for so many of us: Who doesn't know parents who work outrageously hard so their children will be "better off"? This was the case in my home when I was growing up in Poland: Dad often returned from his job as late as 9 or 10 p.m., while Mom once moved halfway across the country for work, coming home to be with us on weekends. It wasn't because we were struggling to make ends meet; rather, it was because of the aspirations of the middle class that were so typical in Poland in the 1990s. Educated people, especially those who spoke a second language, dreamed of transforming their lives and attaining a Western lifestyle. Money was a gateway not just to material goods, but also to travel and other freedoms – followed closely by the pride of an impressive resume. The key to getting there was hard work.

For 10 years I, too, believed that my life needed to revolve around work. For many years, it did – and I don't regret it. I'm proud of what I've achieved. By 22, I was financially independent; at 24, I was able to move abroad and had the ability to support my family when needed. Whenever I could, I matched my work with pleasure, especially traveling. I visited more than 50 countries on four continents, having short adventures in some while living longer-term in others.

But the work always traveled with me – even on vacation, when I definitely should have disconnected from it. Slowly but surely, it was taking a toll on my mental health and well-being. It's a gradual process, one that's easy to overlook. Instead of taking breaks to recharge, I was constantly thinking ahead to the next project, idea, or improvement. It wasn't a punishment or a hardship, though. Work has always been fun for me. I've never had that moment of dreading a Monday; on the contrary, they make me excited: new week, new challenges! The pressure wasn't coming from anywhere but myself: I was convinced, all on my own, that all this work was what it takes to be successful, what you need to do to "make something" of yourself. My dream was to achieve the financial freedom to do whatever I wanted in life, and work was the way to get there.

It's easy to get stuck in the cycle of "work hard, get a reward." Every new contract or professional kudos means a new burst of pride and surge of satisfying dopamine. So we do more, more, more at our jobs, in hopes of getting more, more, more of that reward. Happiness at work means happiness in private life.

Shouldn't it be the other way around?

ACCESSIBILITY TRAP

It's always possible to have too much of a good thing.

As humans, we're not always prepared to admit that what we like might also be hurting us. But for all the flexibility and freedom that comes with remote work, there is a dark side: Burnout.

When the scales tip too far in the wrong direction, it's possible for all the promise of remote work to become a burden or a struggle. Although the true appeal of remote work is more free time and a healthier lifestyle, we can fall into the trap of being constantly online and overworked, which in the long run is counterproductive and dangerous.

Flexible schedules mean you can work whenever you want; but they can also mean you feel like you should always be working.

Having the freedom to work whenever you like can manifest as working all the time or in unhealthy patterns. Setting your own schedule can up-end your divide between work and rest, leading to sleep deprivation, exhaustion, and never being able to truly relax.

The situation is made worse by the constant onslaught of technology — notifications pinging here, emails popping up there — leading to lack of focus and perpetual FOMO. But even if someone asked if you were addicted to your smartphone? Most of us would answer that we have no problem with it. We take 24/7 communication as a given: an element of everyday life and work, a tool for communication with friends and entertainment. The smartphone has become an extension of our hand.

Technological progress' advantages are undeniable, of course, and it has made remote work and the positive lifestyle changes that come with it a viable option for so many more people. But we can't ignore that there's a dark side, too.

Overwork and burnout are among the most frequent topics in labor market research reports ordered in many countries in the second quarter of 2020. Companies that frantically switched to remote set-ups as an emergency option during the pandemic also inadvertently exposed their employees to remote work's unhealthy side. To prove their dedication from afar, people started to work too much and too hard, to the detriment of their mental health.

In a survey of employees of 200 companies, as many as 90% of respondents declared that they were adapting well to remote work. That's encouraging! But more reports are drawing attention to the problem of high expectations and their consequences, with burnout being a major factor. A Gallup study of 7,500 employees found 23 percent felt burned out at work very often or always – if you include those who felt burned out "sometimes," it jumps to 67 percent.

The reasons? Gallup respondents cited the stress of being available 24/7, the lack of free time, unresponsive managers, impossible deadlines and work overload. As many as 41% of remote workers complained about high levels of stress – much more than in the case of office workers (25%). This means that the causes of the disturbing state of affairs is embedded somewhere in the way we're currently making remote work happen.

TOO MUCH TO HANDLE

People working remotely full-time generally report that they are satisfied in their job at higher rates than office workers, even going so far as to say they would rather look for another job than have to abandon their remote status and return to the office.[52] So what's the problem?

In offices, just showing up and sitting in a meeting room is enough to show you're committed and contributing.

> But remote workers feel a need to
> demonstrate their performance in a way
> that can be impossible to achieve.

As a result, they work longer than before and feel more under pressure. More than half say they are putting in over 40 hours a week.[53] Close to half of workers said they were "burned out" after working from home due to a lack of work-life balance.

The distance can create a sense of thinking – whether it's true or not – that people are being ignored or not getting their fair share. One study found that team members who worked from home at least part of the time were 52 percent more likely to feel left out or mistreated, and to have trouble resolving conflict with their co-workers.

Loneliness might sound like a cheesy problem to have, but it's the underlying root of many burnout problems. A survey by Buffer found that 16% of workers found loneliness to be a challenge when working remotely.[54] When we think about some of the problems that people run into when working remotely, feeling lonely almost always comes to the top of the pile. It's natural that employees who are working away from others and in their own setting can from time to time miss the company of their teammates. It's not just a remote issue though, it's also part of a broad, global loneliness trend.

Part of it is being physically isolated at home – fewer people to interact with each day, more time to ourselves. Part of that is about relationships – if you like your co-workers, things tend to run more smoothly. But getting to know your co-workers at all in a fully remote environment is already a challenge. If you can't form healthy bonds with the people you're working alongside, it's easier to feel stressed, mistrustful and to sow doubt among a team.

But with virtual happy hours and Zoom calls every other hour, why are we still feeling so separated? It could be because the bonding process just takes longer over a screen than it does in person. Patience may be part of the solution.

A major cause of the burnout issue is our old friend e-mail. Even despite all of our learning about asynchronous communication, there's still an underlying need to respond right away, a pressure to be always on and show presence, even at the oddest times of the day.

In the COVID-19 era, workers seem to be having more and more trouble separating their work and non work lives. The pandemic seems to have caused those work-life balances issues to jump significantly.[55] This was likely unavoidable, as the issues of transitioning to remote work are facing off against the stress of protecting and caring for our families, friends and loved ones in physically and emotionally draining times. The lines between what we think about at work and at home now seem to be inextricable.

The impact of that is going to show up disproportionately for women. Research suggests that being female was associated with greater family-to-work conflict and greater stress and burnout, whereas being perceived as 'flexible' results in less burnout. These findings support the idea that traditional gender roles and gender bias contribute to burnout, which is especially significant for women working remotely with children at home.

And since things aren't necessarily getting easier, no matter what we wish, we need to find ways to stem burnout as an issue, rather than just waiting it out.

HOW TO DEAL WITH THE BURNOUT DILEMMA

Should we just go back to the office, then? Is this remote experiment not worth the price? Of course not! That's a short-term knee--jerk response to something that has deeper answers. Addressing these issues is key, especially because remote workers seem to be equally or more satisfied with their working conditions as in-office employees.[56] So we have something to fight for!

It's up to employers and employees to find solutions for burnout that will make remote working a sustainable and healthy option for all. Here are some ways to do that:

1 ACKNOWLEDGE YOU HAVE A PROBLEM

Take all the above information into account and trust your employees when they tell you they're at the end of their rope. And if that's not enough, consider that the World Health Organization has declared workplace burnout an officially recognized condition. Countries like France, Denmark and Sweden do recognize burnout syndrome and consider it a legally legitimate reason to take a sick day from work.

How do you know if you're at risk of burnout?

- You often feel tired or lack energy, even though you're otherwise healthy
- You're procrastinating more, avoiding work, or calling in sick more often
- You're making more mistakes or the quality of your work has dropped
- It takes longer to finish your work, even the "easy" tasks
- You've developed unhealthy habits, like skipping meals and exercise, or avoiding social time with friends and family
- You work all day, but still feel like it's not enough

Pay close attention to such symptoms, and if you notice them, act immediately.

2 SET BOUNDARIES

After a 2015 report found information overload was harming the working-age population, France's "Right to Disconnect" became a law. Today, companies there with at least 50 workers must have policies in place to allow staff to disconnect from work technology after hours.

Even when it's not legally required, a major way to prevent burnout is to encourage (and enforce) the notion that remote workers should disconnect as much as possible. Consider setting up official offline hours or organizing a workshop on setting clear boundaries, and make sure managers set a good example for the rest of your employees. (After all, if the boss isn't actually taking time to disconnect, too, his team will assume it's just a trap and keep up their 24/7 pace to match his.)

Part of that is letting go of the idea that everything needs to be handled immediately. Not everything needs to have the same level of urgency; as a result, it's important to focus on prioritization. If you set clear priorities for your team, they'll be less overwhelmed and less likely to burn out. Not everything needs to be an emergency – some things can wait.

Another issue is regular holidays. I feel strange advising managers to encourage their employees to NOT work, but ... well, here we are. Too many people ignore taking proper vacation time, even when it's offered to them or they need it. Sometimes it's because the company culture makes vacation-takers feel like slackers; other times, we are so overwhelmed by the amount of responsibilities that putting them aside even for a moment seems unthinkable.

However, without regular rest and isolation from work, we will be doomed to frustration and exhaustion. Even Harvard studies say that never taking a vacation can mess with your motivation. If you're working weekends, or continuing to answer emails from your beach vacay while ducking out of the sun to see your laptop screen for a quick check-in, you're not mentally disconnecting and recharging. Even I find myself doing this at times. Therefore, before a vacation, I always delete work-related applications from my phone.

And that recharging is, ironically, how we end up doing our best work. A 2018 survey by the American Psychological

Association finds that 70 percent of workers are in a better mood, with more positivity and energy, after their vacation and a staggering 60 percent end up feeling more productive upon their return.

70% of employees say they feel their best after a holiday, and 60% say that's when they're most productive.[57]

At Zillow, for example, they've decided to give everyone an extra day off and even encourage people to take the SAME day off so no one would feel pressured to keep answering email or attending meetings just because everyone else was "on" as normal. And, most importantly, company leadership joined in to set the right example. Even a policy of Summer Fridays can be enough to let people recharge their mental batteries.

In addition to holidays, it is also very important to make sure that everyone takes breaks from time to time. Studies have shown it's a surefire way to boost mood and morale among workers.[58] Some companies have found people who spend all day in video meetings can't get away from their live-streamed workspaces long enough to use the toilet or grab a cup of coffee, without feeling overly conspicuous.[59] When your way of working means you can't take a bathroom break, things have gone awry. Remind your team to take breaks throughout the day and don't punish employees who don't immediately respond to your messages.

Also designate a clear end of the working day. Getting caught in the trap of "Just one more thing and I'll log out" means you'll never turn off your laptop. Deal with the fact that no matter how much you do, there's always something that can wait for tomorrow.

3 LEARN TO SAY NO

This one seems obvious, of course, but like many things is easier in theory than in practice. Because often, when we're being asked to add one more task to our to-do list or one more responsibility to our plate, we're in a position where we think a) there will be negative consequences if we say no or b) it's something we actually want to do! There's the trickiest part – how do you say no to something that is reasonable, or desirable?

One smart strategy for navigating the never-ending "just one more thing!" impulse: instead of saying no, say "let's talk priorities." By letting the person who is asking for more know that you're not giving them a blanket negative response, you're opening the door to a discussion of why this is important and also how it fits into both of your respective workloads. It's possible this frank discussion will lead to a trade-off in which you cede one responsibility to make way for this new one; or, it could make clear that the other items on your to-do list are actually more important and the new bit will just have to wait. Making it clear that if they want you to do X, you'll have to NOT do Y can paint a clearer picture about what the options really are.

Sometimes saying "yes, but ..." can be as effective as a "no." And at the end of the day, you want to find ways to say yes to the things that matter without exceeding your capacity for quality work.

4 FIGHT LONELINESS

Digital nomad life means constantly meeting new people, working in a co-working space with others to bounce ideas off, and other lifestyle structures that can help overcome loneliness. But working from a home office can be more limiting. In that case, it's important to try working from outside the home semi-regularly. This could mean a local co-working space, a cafe, a friend's house, or anywhere else where you can casually interact with others. Try setting aside a day a week to do so, or ask your employer for an allowance to work from a co-working space if you are worried about costs.

Virtual meetings can also help reduce the feeling of loneliness. Try keeping the video on – I know, it's tempting to just go audio so no one sees your bedhead and messy house, but being face to face fosters connection and makes things more personal.

Additionally, try working in "social time" during online meetings – meaning set aside time that isn't about the projects and tasks of the day, but instead about social interaction. Literally five minutes at the beginning or end of a virtual meeting is enough to talk about personal matters, joke and just be yourself. If you have fun, try to arrange separate, non-work related meetings, such as an evening game session.

And if you're in a place where gathering at a co-working isn't an option, try doing it online. Virtual co-working spaces are great places to meet people with a similar lifestyle – a good remedy for loneliness. You can take part in collaborative work sessions, social meetings or educational classes – all without leaving your home office.

Another way to avoid the feeling of loneliness,is to join groups focused around common interests: sports, hobbies and all activities not related to deadlines and business projects. Getting to know people who are equally passionate about your interests can be therapeutic and fight loneliness. Believe me, it works!!

5 TAKE CARE OF YOUR HEALTH: PHYSICAL AND MENTAL

You can get sick from too much work – literally. Mental stress and pressure can even manifest as physical ailments. Overwork and burnout can contribute to high blood pressure, weight gain, alcoholism, substance abuse, and many other serious issues. Even just living a sedentary lifestyle takes its toll.

The price for this is high – in the United States, estimates suggest burnout can cost up to $190 billion USD in health costs. But there are ways companies can support their teams' physical wellness. The virtual world opens the doors to online and on-demand yoga and fitness classes, as well as services that promote meditation, mental health, healthy eating and diet, and solutions for anxiety and stress relief. Subscriptions to these online services, or a spend-it-yourself budget benefit, can encourage maxed-out employees to find the option that works best for them. Additionally, team-building challenges around physical health, or scheduled group meets for meditation or clarity building can make people feel united and supported in pursuing healthy habits.

Not so long ago, meditation was seen as a new age-y trend, but today even the top people in the business world recognize its benefits.

Microsoft's Bill Gates said in 2018 that it was "a great tool for improving my focus" and something he enjoys a few times per week[60]; Twitter's Jack Dorsey and billionaire hedge fund manager Ray Dalio have cited it as part of their everyday routine. There are many apps that can help you get started with meditation practices – try Headspace or Calm, for example.

6 TAKE CARE OF EACH OTHER

We all want recognition – both for our work and simply for who we are. Research shows that companies with a recognition program increase engagement and productivity.[61] It does not necessarily have to be a wide-ranging and detailed program – sometimes a simple "thank you!" or "great job!" is enough. In a virtual environment, we often don't know what others think about our contributions or the quality of our work; any appreciation for a job well done can have a positive impact.

FIRST-HAND

Ryan Burke

One of the most experienced experts in building remote sales teams in the world, Burke was included in the Top 50 Sales Leaders list of the British Sales Confidence ranking. He's currently Chief Revenue Officer at Qatalog, previously a longtime Senior VP International at InVision..

When I first joined InVision in 2014, it was one of the first 'work from anywhere' companies in the world. I was very skeptical of the setup having been a traditional 'in office' type leader. In my tenure at InVision we grew from 30 employees to over 850, making it the largest fully remote company in the world at that time, so I've had experience with remote long before Covid stimulated the massive shift to where we are today.

Put simply, I love the ability to work from anywhere and to spend more time with my family.

But it isn't always easy and it requires deliberate changes. Forget the changes in how you work. There is now a SaaS tool to address any gap in employee communication or collaboration you can dream up. The changes required are around your frame of mind and how you manage the separation of your work and personal lives. And to be clear, it's no longer work/life balance, not even close. It's purely work/life integration – for better or worse.

When I think about this new blended reality, to me it's the edges that buffer these two worlds that are the most affected. Those small transitions from one context to the next. And it's how you prioritize and manage these 'edges' to maintain the right level of connectedness, transition, and inclusion that helps you maintain a healthy mental state.

Sometimes that edge may be a casual conversation after a meeting on the walk back to your desk or a coffee at the airport with a colleague after a long trip. In an office culture, it is a built-in natural time to decompress, to have that breather outside of the intensity of your work. Turns out that some of those connections can actually be the fabric that helps make those transitions from work to personal context – and back – tolerable. In some cases those casual connections can become the secret sauce that defines a 'culture' of a company.

When you go remote, you lose some of those soft edges. With Covid, we lost even more.

Part of the reason I ended up getting a trainer in London was to have another piece of connectivity, a softer edge between work and life. Exercise and working out is great (in theory), but running from my desk to the basement to crank on weights and get it off my to-do list while my mind was still racing wasn't giving the exercise enough space to work for my mental state. Having a person I liked catching up with working out alongside me helped me to transition from 5 hours of Zoom calls to a workout that was actually helpful for my mind and body.

Finding ways to navigate those edges is the key. In a remote world you enjoy the benefit of removing the natural hard edges that split work and life, restricting personal experiences. The commute to work, seeing your kids only early and late in the day (or sometimes neither), the travel time involved in your family holiday. These are the barriers no one misses. In fact, when I look back sometimes I wonder how I even let those become an accepted part of my day. The negatives that limit time with who you cherish most can be deteriorating to mental well-being and severely compound any stress from your actual job.

But it can be hard to make the transition from work stress to home life when you don't have that commute to decompress. When you're head-down in QBRs and your kids barge in eager to tell you a story, it's natural to shoo them away. But that's a missed positive moment. Knowing how to manage that edge, that transition, that's the hard part. I started creating small projects and activities I could quickly pick up with my kids in an instant. Puzzles, sports. We even made a movie as family – an ongoing project we dipped in and out of. If a meeting ends 15 minutes early – we can connect for a few. The barriers are down, the expected schedules are fluid. I can spend an hour outside playing football with the kids on a beautiful afternoon and work a few extra hours after they go to bed. Those are the times when having those hard edges removed mean everything, as soon as you become comfortable with the integration of the two worlds.

For me, making sure I truly take advantage of 'work from anywhere' versus 'work from home' helps me. We push our holidays a bit longer, even if I am working, so that after work I can walk straight to the beach and be with my family in a rewarding environment. Not every holiday has to be extravagant because it's our long-planned vacation. We take smaller, spontaneous 'adventures' and all benefit from my flexibility.

Forget productivity. People, and companies, now have to rethink the way they feel connected, included, and supported. And how they manage the edges.

CHAPTER 11:

WHAT'S NEXT?
10 TRENDS FOR THE
REMOTE FUTURE

Seeing up close just how remote work is impacting the world, I would always feel a bit .... unsatisfied. Only one group of people seemed to benefit from the changes: the employees of companies that dared to step into the remote world. The revolution was spreading, but it wasn't mainstream enough to give most people the freedom of choice. And employers who didn't trust their employees were holding things back. But with the sudden arrival of the pandemic, the world had a chance to accelerate things.

By spring 2021, we can say with certainty that we will never go back to the "normal," state that preceded the pandemic. This is (mostly) good news! We have a unique opportunity to influence and shape the future, to decide what our new "normal" should look like. By "we" I don't just mean businesses and workers, but also the "us" that includes parents, citizens, community members, and more. The decisions we will make now will impact not just ourselves, but also future generations and the shape of society as we know it. (No pressure, right?)

The spread of remote work will change not only the professional sphere, but also force us to reevaluate and redefine many of our social norms and habits, and will have massive consequences for the economy and the environment. Here, I present a subjective list of 10 major trends we can expect to see as remote work expands. believe that this is what a new, better world can look like.

1. **Co-living:** Living in communes 2.0
2. **Slowmadism:** The migratory birds of digital capitalism
3. **Global Labor Redefined:** Silicon Valley anywhere you want it

4. **Exodus from the Metropolis:** Rethinking and rediscovering livable locations

5. **Head of Remote:** Captains of the remote revolution

6. **TGI-Thursday:** The four-day work week

7. **Climate of Change:** Remote work in the fight against the climate crisis

8. **World Without Barriers:** New visions of diversity and inclusivity

9. **Remote Feminism:** The new dimensions of equality

10. **Stakeholder Capitalism:** Profit isn't all that matters

1 CO-LIVING REVOLUTION: LIVING IN COMMUNES 2.0

The idea of a group of unrelated people living together is nothing new. For many years, people who share common values have created "dormitories for adults" all over the world – places where they lived together, spent their free time, and often also worked. The most recent incarnation of this kind of group living is what we're calling *co-living*.

There are two approaches to co-living. The first is co-living in big cities, which offers an alternative to very expensive private apartment rentals. This trend has been growing in the United States for several years, especially in cities like New York and San Francisco, where housing costs are astronomical. The second is co-living in tropical corners of the world, such as the Indonesian island of Bali. They are refuges for digital nomads who want to be a part of a community and join up with like-minded peers for a part of their journeys around the globe.

I predict more and more people will turn to co-living, especially when looking for ways to travel or live outside of their home countries. For example, Selina – a hotel chain geared toward digital nomads – has expanded to dozens of facilities on three continents. Companies like Outpost and Outsite offer members access to hand-picked co-living sites, communities and work-friendly amenities. And plenty of other people will create their own ad-hoc coliving groups as they settle for long or short term in desirable destinations.

> For many people, this community is crucial. It is part of treating travel as a long-term lifestyle, rather than just a way of enjoying a short-term vacation.

2 SLOWMADISM: THE MIGRATORY BIRDS OF DIGITAL CAPITALISM

When the pandemic is at least partially contained, and the borders are opened again, many people will take the opportunity to join the ranks of *slowmads*. Until now, work and travel have been linked mainly to the already mentioned digital nomads: mostly freelancers who left their old jobs and lives to set off into the world, changing locations frequently and casually. With slowmadism, a new movement is gaining steam. It's powered by people who want to be able to move freely for a few weeks or months to a selected place in the world, to temporarily live there and work remotely.

Slowmads won't necessarily have to give up their permanent jobs or turn their lives upside down, leaving home behind with nothing but a backpack. As remote work becomes more popular and more normalized, full-time employees of all kinds of more traditional companies will find themselves with unprecedented freedom and the opportunity to explore new places around the world. For some, it will mean a way to escape unpleasant winters; for others, it represents a chance for adventure and cultural exploration that runs deeper than traditional tourism. Still others see it as an opportunity to support communities in less-developed regions of the world, not just by spending money in their locales but also by sharing their professional skills and knowledge with the people who live there and might not usually have access to that kind of experience.

More countries are simplifying the legal and tax formalities for longer-term visitors, and slowmads are poised to reap the benefits of these initiatives. Governments around the world are starting to recognize – and value – remote workers, and beginning to issue new visa options to suit them or entice them to nations that might otherwise be overlooked. In 2020, nomad-friendly visas were introduced by the Bahamas, Greece, Georgia and the United Arab Emirates, among others. And this is just the beginning of new options for remote workers, who will be increasingly appealing to the tourism industry.

If you want to try this way of life and wonder where to start in the world, check out Nomad List, which aggregates information about life and work in various corners of the globe. It was created for digital nomads, but now it will also be useful for those who prefer the prefix "slow". https://nomadlist.com/

3 GLOBAL LABOR REDEFINED: SILICON VALLEY ANYWHERE YOU WANT IT

The year 2021 means a redefinition of the boundaries of the labor market, which gives employers new opportunities. Companies that have once refused to hire remote workers have now changed their minds. Many employers – Facebook, Salesforce, and Shopify are just a few examples – have introduced revolutionary remote work programs in the last several months. That means that where you live and where you work no longer need to be connected. It's a win--win situation – employers get to draw from a broader pool of prospects, and workers get access to a wider variety of opportunities.

This also means major changes to how we think about wages. Should a graphic designer from a small city in Portugal, for example, earn the same as an equally experienced designer doing the same job for the same company while living in San Francisco? Typically our Portuguese friend would make less based on the market and cost of living in each city; but will that be fair once remote work is the new normal? Companies will have to decide not only whether salaries should be more uniform, but whether they should be more public. Pay transparency is a growing trend. Companies like GitLab and Buffer have been calculating salaries for years using publicly available calculators. As remote work scales larger, will other companies follow in their footsteps?

Employers will have to think seriously about this and many other questions. And no matter what answers they ultimately find, we can expect a revolution in the field of remuneration. It's time to go all-in and introduce total wage standardization and transparency. Salaries should be based on a clear and publicly disc-losed methodology. These changes will likely lead to far-reaching consequences and help close the pay gap between wealthy and poor communities, and between male and female employees.

4 EXODUS FROM THE METROPOLIS: RETHINKING AND REDISCOVERING LIVABLE LOCATIONS

One of the greatest advantages of working remotely is the opportunity to abandon the daily commute, that hellish ordeal of time-sucking traffic jams that ate up hours of our time each week and hurt our health by increasing our stress levels, our blood pressure, and our weight.

When work is no longer centered around a physical location, traditional cities and the patterns of life within them start to change. At the same time, the pandemic has altered the landscape of cities in significant ways – and probably for good. If we don't need to be in an office, then we don't need to live near the office .... which means no need for commuting to city centers every day. As people seek more comfortable living conditions – and more space while working home – the suburbs and the countryside will start to usurp some of the financial and cultural importance now rooted in major metropolises. Bill Gates even predicted an exodus of high-earning workers from dynamic cities such as San Francisco and Seattle long before it actually happened. After all, a spacious multi--bedroom house would be more alluring to a lot of people than the tiny studio apartments they're putting up with to be close to work.

This could mean positive things for city life, as those who remain in each urban center will be the ones most invested in its cultural life and invested in its social community, rather than people forced to live there by virtue of their jobs.

And it also means a coming renaissance for small towns and villages once derided for being "in the middle of nowhere." Once living in these smaller locations doesn't require sacrificing career growth and income opportunities, they'll become more appealing to people seeking an escape from the noise, crowds and pollution of city life. Regions that have experienced a massive exodus to cities in recent decades might end up seeing the trend reverse. In 2018, for example, Tulsa, Oklahoma – a relatively small city by American standards with a population of 400,000 – began a subsidy program that offered remote workers a bonus package of $10,000 if they relocated there. Tulsa might not be the hottest city in the U.S., but the offer fired up interest in a big way: as many as 10,000 applications were reportedly submitted for the 100 slots in the first edition of the initiative. It's a sign of an important shift: in the age of remote work, cities and towns no longer have to battle for corporations in hopes that landing company HQ will lure in new residents ... now, they can cater to the interests of individual workers instead.

#5 HEAD OF REMOTE: CAPTAINS OF THE REMOTE REVOLUTION

Until recently, there were very few remote-first companies, and fewer still that employed more than a few dozen full-time workers. Those pioneering companies that had 100 or more remote workers had to experiment with the best ways to run their internal operations, a trial-and-error effort involving a mishmash of individuals from across a broad spectrum of teams, most notably from the Human Resources department. Now, companies that are embracing their remoteness are seeking to centralize decisions about how location-independent operations should work and finding their own Heads of Remote to establish best remote practices and manage the workforce transitions. Darren Murph – whose input you read in Chapter 9 – was once curiously unique as GitLab's Head of Remote; now, more businesses are looking to hire specialists to take charge of their remote revolutions. By the end of 2020, even Facebook and Quora had announced they were recruiting for positions that would be responsible for taking their teams remote-first.

> Chief Remote Officer, Director of Remote, Head of Hybrid – such titles will be seen more and more in the coming years.

As organizations with larger and larger workforces shift into hybrid and remote models, the people in these groundbreaking positions will have to not only manage the complicated tasks of transitioning old-school companies into the new world, but also finding ways to ensure that the logistical and cultural changes that come with it are long-lasting and constantly improved.

6 TGI-THURSDAY?: EMBRACING THE FOUR-DAY WORK WEEK

In recent years, companies have experimented with the idea of the four-day work week ... and the results are very promising. The Japanese branch of Microsoft implemented a monthly pilot program in 2019, reducing working hours while keeping wages at the previous level, and found productivity jumped 40 percent, while company costs dropped (the electricity bill, for example, went down by 23 percent.)

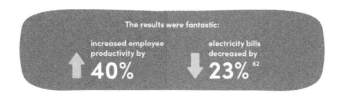

It's not just corporations – governments and others are also experimenting with shorter days and weeks. The city of Gothenburg, Sweden, ran a two-year pilot program allowing nurses to work six-hour days; they found participants had increased job satisfaction and better overall health. (Interestingly, less fatigue at work led to an increase in physical activity in private life by as much as 24%.[63]) In May 2020, New Zealand Prime Minister Jacinda Ardern encouraged businesses to introduce a shorter work week to boost productivity and improve employees' work-life balance. In response, the New Zealand branch of Unilever announced in January 2021 that its team of 81 people would move to a four-day week for one year; if the results are good, the initiative would expand to cover the company's 155,000 employees worldwide. Also in January 2021, Spain announced a subsidy program with a budget of €50 million to incentivize companies to try a four-day week to see it's impact on productivity and mental health. And Buffer decided to extend its pandemic-inspired pilot program through the end of 2021.[64] Inevitably, more businesses will start to make the shift; the impact on how we work and live will be huge.

7 CLIMATE OF CHANGE: REMOTE WORK AND THE FIGHT AGAINST THE CLIMATE CRISIS

The impending climate crisis is finally getting the attention it deserves, as dramatic headlines highlight increasingly frequent and terrible wildfires, floods and storms wrecking havoc around the world. made headlines quite recently. And all the research points to things getting much worse.

In the autumn of 2020, Ola and I saw with our own eyes just how brutal these storms, worsened by climate change, can be. A series of deadly and devastating typhoons barrelled through our home base of Hội An on Vietnam's central coast, followed by weeks of dangerous flooding. Vietnam's economy was ranked 13th in the world among those most affected by climate change.[65]

The good news is that more and more people are realizing the importance of changing the course of the planet and saving the environment, as best we can, before we're doomed. One way to do that may be changing the way we work.

When the world came to a halt with the outbreak of the COVID-19 pandemic, the average daily emissions of these

harmful substances decreased by 17% compared to the correspon-
ding month of 2019.[66] It is definitive proof that redefining how we
work and live can have a positive impact on Earth's environment.
The spread of remote work means fewer miles traveled as video
conferencing cancels out daily commutes and routine business
trips. Office energy consumption – which, together with commercial spaces such as shops and restaurants, is responsible for as
much as 6.6% of global emissions[67] – will also decrease.

We must bear in mind that not everything about remote work
is good for the environment; for example, location independence
could increase air travel, which contributes a small but rising amount to overall global emissions. Plus, our reliance on digital devices
and subsequent data storage on global servers is consuming massive amounts of electricity and contributing to the carbon emissions
crisis.[68] As a result, companies and governments need to consider
sustainable development part of their future strategies as remote
work spreads. And individuals should use some of the time fre-
ed up by the benefits of a remote-work lifestyle to get involved in
countering the climate crisis, whether by educating themselves or
supporting local pro-environment initiatives.

8 WORLD WITHOUT BARRIERS: NEW VISIONS OF DIVERSITY AND INCLUSIVENESS

Exclusion and discrimination against people based on race, sexual orientation, age, and other factors is a major problem in the
professional sphere. Remote work gives us a brand new chance
to fight inequalities, as it opens the doors to people who would

normally be passed over or who might not have access to the same job opportunities.

Employers have started to take the issues of social diversity and inclusiveness more seriously – initially it may have been for public image reasons, but more and more it's about actual financial impact. According to the Harvard Business Review analysis, companies with a more diverse management staff generate 10% higher revenues[69]. A study by the Boston Consulting Group found that homogeneous ones.[70]

> More diverse teams are almost **twice as innovative.**"

Remote reality opens up new opportunities for employers in the sphere of diversity and inclusiveness. Though conversations in the business world of the past mostly just paid lip service to potential solutions to diversity issues, changing attitudes are putting pressure on companies to take action, and remote work is providing the tools and opportunities to make it happen. Remote work enables the recruitment of people who have been routinely neglected, including people with physical disabilities, people who live far from economic centers and can't relocate, and people who live in parts of the world with limited or under-developed opportunities for their skills. Meanwhile, more companies – among them Pinterest, Bank of America, and eBay – are appointing people to actively implement strategies that increase inclusivity and diversity. More will surely follow.

9 REMOTE FEMINISM:
NEW DIMENSIONS OF EQUALITY

Women are still faced with the age-old struggle between career and motherhood. But remote work offers new ways to overcome the struggles facing working moms. It can also lead to a more equitable division of domestic labor, such as household chores and child rearing. As more work takes place outside the office structure, more women will have opportunities to stay in the game and climb the corporate ladder. Businesses will also benefit from it. A Credit Suisse Research Institute study shows that companies with at least one female board member have a statistically higher return on investment and higher average revenue growth than those with all-male boards.[72]

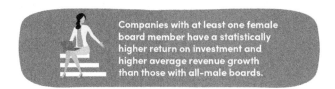

Companies with at least one female board member have a statistically higher return on investment and higher average revenue growth than those with all-male boards.

This is just one of many studies that suggest a world with women at the helm can be not only more empathetic, but also more business-efficient. And though about 77% of the board members of Fortune 500 companies are still men, remote work is making a dent in female participation in the upper echelons of the corporate world. According to Remote.co, women are presidents, founders or executive directors of 28% of remote companies – that's more than four times the rate of Fortune 500 companies.[73] So we can hope that remote work opens a new chapter in the history of equality.

10 STAKEHOLDER CAPITALISM: PROFIT ISN'T ALL THAT MATTERS

Our first haven after leaving Poland was the United States. And though, like so many others, we arrived smitten with the idea of the "American dream," over the years we've found its charms have faded. For all of the rhetoric about freedom and opportunity, America also suffers greatly from problems of inequality brought on by extreme capitalism in which the desire to maximize profits at all costs drives decision making.

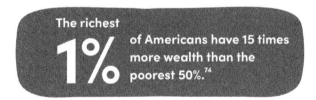

The business world, forever focused on profit optimization, needs to take a closer look at social impact. I do not want to say that everything has gone wrong – since the end of World War II, life expectancy and overall quality of life has risen around the world. The problem is that we divide this increasingly larger cake less and less fairly. Massive income disparity, growing rates of homelessness in places like San Francisco, and other problems show the old "American dream" may be unattainable, even within her own borders.

Perhaps it's time to consider the dream's Version 2.0 – a way of rethinking our ideals in the wake of the challenges of 2021. Now is the moment for critical reflection and change. If capitalism as we know it isn't supporting society, maybe we need to rethink how it works. According to Edelman Trust Barometer results published in January 2020, respondents in 22 out of 28 countries surveyed believe that capitalism causes more harm than good worldwide (56% of the 34,000 people surveyed agreed with this claim.[75])

Therefore, it is possible that in the post-pandemic reality a new incarnation of this system will come to the fore – *stakeholder capitalism*. In such a model, companies aim to meet the needs not just of their own shareholders, but of society and the world as a whole. It's not a new concept: its outlines were initially presented at the first World Economic Forum in Davos in 1971. It is an alternative to the two main variants of this system to date: shareholder capitalism, in which the ultimate goal of each company is to maximize profits; and state capitalism, where the course of the economy is charted by the government (this is the case, for example, in China).

Under stakeholder capitalism, it is important not only to maximize the profits of the enterprise, but to put the welfare of employees, business partners, society and the planet on equal footing. Firms should change the way they make decisions by following a new guiding principle – "creating shared value", including "environmental, social and good corporate governance."[76] In such a model, corporate social responsibility stops consisting of empty PR slogans and starts being a meaningful and effective way to function.

I've pointed out time and again in this book that remote work has the capacity to make life better for individuals; but it's also uniquely suited to supporting the kind of economic and value system changes I'm spelling out here. In that way, remote work can truly make the world a better place.

EPILOGUE

A year has passed since we moved to Hoi An. Vietnam, once intended to be just a short phase of the journey we started on four years ago, has become our new home. By living and working here, we've come to know this town not just through the tourist lens of Instagram beauty, but through the more realistic prism of everyday life.

We did not plan to stay so long, but fate ordered that we spend the pandemic in the second safest country in the world (just behind New Zealand.) The borders remain tightly closed, any returnees or business experts arriving on rare, coveted special visas are whisked into government quarantine on arrival, and masks are a common sight, even without formal laws demanding them. Whenever a new coronavirus case emerges in the country, contact tracing and strict isolation measures strangle its spread.

Even in these strange times, Hoi An continues to charm us every day. It is not without reason that the name of the city literally means "a peaceful meeting place." Tourists are practically nonexistent these days, so every evening we can walk almost alone in the now-quiet (and still UNESCO designated) Old Town. Beautiful brick and wooden houses, quaint streets and narrow alleys, red and yellow lanterns – sometimes I have the impression that we moved to the 18th century. The surrounding beaches are also nearly empty most days. Locals eagerly await the return of tourists (and their money), but even despite the financial hardships of the pandemic and blocked borders, they remain empathetic, helpful, and kind. We love our everyday life, though it is so different from the life of the town's native residents, who spend their days tending to rice fields, feeding water buffaloes and fleets of ducks, and sailing out in basket boats to catch fish and shrimp.

It would be easy to sink into the peace and beauty of this place and do nothing; but instead, we spend our days mostly hard at work. In the dawn of the pandemic, we set up shop at our favorite co-working space; later, we turned to working from our home.

The work crises that plagued me in 2020 have been resolved, and we've stopped focusing our efforts on the draining work of finding investors. (I've stopped chanting "We are a promising startup, we will find another round of financing soon!" in my sleep.) Instead, we've turned our attention to laying the foundations of a healthy business. The result? Remote-how now earns for itself. In addition to the Academy of Remote Work, we have created a marketplace platform, which connects remote work experts with companies looking for consulting and operational support. This is something much easier to scale, and at the same time a solution that allows me to rely more on technology – instead of holding meetings from morning to night.

Apart from work, we still have many opportunities to explore the area and, from time to time, organize trips to other parts of Vietnam – our favorite so far has been an epic motorbike trip that brought us through Ha Giang province up to the Chinese border and through the breathtaking mountains and valleys of the north. These moments charge our batteries like nothing else.

We also find time for inner exploration. Ola discovered an artistic talent within herself: the long hidden soul of a painter. And after a year and a half of remote work, she was promoted and is now responsible for the development of her company in international markets. Who would have thought that such a feat would be achieved by a person who, just a few years ago, did not like talking to strangers at all? And I? I have fulfilled a few dreams that have followed me for a long time. Until now, my writing experience has been mostly limited to composing business e-mails; but I truly had fun preparing this book. I've also been reminded that it's not just my job that can offer that powerful dose of dopamine. In high school, I watched with jealousy as friends drove crowds in Warsaw clubs wild from behind a DJ console. Now, since receiving a DJ set of my own for my 30th birthday, I've had the thrill of learning how to do it for myself. (So far my listeners are mostly water buffalos and chickens.)

Although the world may never return to "normal," and though it may seem that we're stuck on the sidelines, it feels as if we are at the very center of this great change. Every day I have conversations with representatives of companies scattered around the globe. One thing is clear to everyone: the time for a revolution has come. The moment when it is necessary to redefine what has been the norm until now. There is excitement combined with fear in everyone's voices. They feel like they are becoming part of the story. Co-creators of the new reality in which companies will finally start to trust their employees and stop controlling them. In which work will be judged on the basis of results, not the hours spent in front of the computer. And in which openness and transparency will become the foundations of our organizational culture.

We cannot allow old habits to get in the way of a better, more sustainable world. The remote revolution isn't just about changing the way we work – it's an opportunity for each and every one of us to change the way we live our lives. For more positive vibrations, more control over what our days look like. We will decide how we live, not our employers.

A year ago, no one could have imagined a world that looked like this, or that change would come so suddenly and on such a massive scale. But out of the darkness and drama of a difficult 2020, we've drawn the unique opportunity to be free, to choose where and how we work.

So it's time to start working remotely – and to finally live a normal life.

Hội An, Vietnam, February 2021

WITH GRATITUDE

Thank you to my parents, Monika and Witek, for their great support during the entire process of creating this book: from the concept phase, when they both commented on my ideas (often very bluntly!), to working on the structure (Mom, thanks for the idea with stories about morning coffee!) to comments on the finished text. Dad says he has never read a book so many times before, and he reads at least one a week.

Thank you to my wife and my best friend Ola. You were the greatest psychological support for me and you helped me a lot in terms of content, especially as an experienced remote employee. Also, thank you for bringing a dose of healthy skepticism to the whole project. I'm glad that it only took until two weeks before the book went to print for you to announce, "Okay, finally, I like it."

Thanks to Amanda McGrath, who joined in to support me operationally on the book. Your journalistic flair and 10 years of experience in the editorial office of The Washington Post have done their job. When we met for the first coffee at our favorite 145 Espresso Cafe in Hội An, you couldn't believe it when I presented you with the deadlines we had to meet. However, a miracle happened – largely due to your very hard work, for which I am sincerely grateful!

I would like to thank my friends who bravely accompanied me in the whole creative process. Without your honesty, the book would not be the same – it was brutal, but it was meant to be!

- Magda Sowierszenko and Marek Grygier, thank you for the expert texts in the "First hand" section and for supporting me with your vast knowledge of remote work.
- My closest high school friends – Łukasz Lisicki and Olgierd Syczewski – thank you for your humanistic talent, broad horizons and consistent care that I do not drift away too much into the world of my visions.
- I would like to thank Julia Berg for the academic and journalistic advice that helped this book take shape. Now I keep my fingers crossed for your doctoral dissertation!
- I would also like to thank my friend and literary agent Piotr Wawrzeńczyk. It was he who in November 2019 decided to take a risk and let me try my hand at writing. This story – like many similar stories – could have ended on the very evening it began. But a year and a half later, it finally found its happy end! It would not have been possible without you and your constant support. And this is just the beginning!
- Thank you to all Remote Pioneers who have decided to share in this book their many years of experience working for the best remote companies in the world. I am honored that you decided to get involved in this project! Remote kudos for Barbie Brewer, Dorota

Piotrowska, Chase Warrington, Mark Tippin, Spencer Waldron, Darren Murph, and Ryan Burke.

I would like to thank Monika Mielke, Dorota Jabłońska, Bartek Kaftan and the entire Wielka Litera publishing house for their trust and for enduring the turbulent creative process until the very end. I'm sorry for being so annoying; in my defense, I can only say: "I warned you!" The support I got from you was fantastic and I am very, very grateful for it! Until the next project! :)

FOOTNOTES

1. Christopher Ingraham, *Nine days on the road. Average commute time reached a new record last year*, "The Washington Post," Oct. 7, 2019, accessed: https://www.washingtonpost.com/business/2019/10/07/nine-days-road-average-commute-time-reached-new-record-last-year/

2. Sheila McClear, *These are the Top 10 reasons people want to work remotely*, November 25, 2019, accessed: https://www.theladders.com/career-advice/these-are-the-top-10-reasons-people- want-to-work-remotely

3. *We Asked 8,000 People How They Want To Work Post-COVID-19. Here Are 5 Things They Told Us That Will Likely Change the World of Work Forever*, June 30, 2020, accessed: https://www.adeccogroup.com/future- of-work/latest-insights/we-asked-8000-people-how-they-want-to-work-post-covid-19-here-are-5-things-they-told-us-that-will /

4. *The Millennial Mind Goes to Work, discussion transcript at Bentley University*, November 12, 2014, accessed: https://www.bentley.edu/news/millennial-mind-goes-work

5. *Millennials. Fueling The Experience Economy*, available at: http://eventbrite-s3.s3.amazonaws.com/marketing/Millennials_Research/Gen_PR_Final.pdf

6. *4 in 5 Employees Want Benefits or Perks More Than a Pay Raise*; Glassdoor Employment Confidence Survey (Q3 2015), October 2, 2015, accessed: https://www.glassdoor.com/blog/ecs-q3-2015/

7. *New trend report: Generation Z: Building a Better Normal*, December 2, 2020, access: https://intelligence.wundermanthompson.com/2020/12/new-trend-report-generation-z-building-a-better-normal/

8. *The 2021 State of Remote Work, report by Buffer,* accessed: https://buffer.com/2021-state-of-remote-work

9. Nathan Allen, *The Pioneers of Modern Remote Work*, November 10, 2020, accessed: https://wrkfrce.com/the-pioneers-of-modern-remote-work/

10. Fadeke Adegbuyi, *8 Lessons from the Best Remote Companies in the World*, accessed: https://blog.doist.com/lessons-remote-companies/

11. Matt Mullenweg, *Gradually, Then Suddenly*, May 21, 2020, accessed: https://ma.tt/2020/05/gradually-then-suddenly/

12. Joni Sweet, *Travel And Exploration Spark Happiness, Study Suggests,* "Forbes," May 22, 2020, accessed: https://www.forbes.com/sites/jonisweet/2020/05/22/travel-increases-happiness-study-finds/?sh=58875b1e6793

13. *Personality Type Indicator, My Personality Test*, accessed: https://my-personality-test.com/personality-type-indicator

14. *The IWG Global Workspace Survey*, 2019

15. Nicholas Bloom et al., *Does Working from Home Work? Evidence from a Chinese Experiment*, March 2013, accessed: https://www.gsb.stanford.edu/faculty-research/working-papers/does-working-home-work- evidence-chinese-experiment

16. Daniel James, *8 Work At Home Statistics You Need To Know*, September 30, 2015, accessed: https://www.business2community.com/ human-resources/8-work-at-home-statistics-you-need-to-know-01342583#7xiU7H7RLgExYxaD.97

17. *Flexjobs Mental Health America Survey*, August 28, 2020, accessed: https://www.flexjobs.com/blog/post/flexjobs-mha-mental-health-workplace-pandemic/

18. *The Cost of Replacing an Employee and the Role of Financial Wellness*, January 15, 2016, accessed: https://www.enrich.org/blog/The-true-cost-of- employee-turnover-financial-wellness-enrich

19. *FlexJobs Survey: Productivity, Work-Life Balance Improves During Pandemic*, Sept. 21, 2020, accessed: https://www.flexjobs.com/blog/post/survey-productivity-balance-improve-during-pandemic-remote-work/

20. Sarah Jensen Clayton, *6 Signs Your Corporate Culture Is a Liability,* "Harvard Business Review," December 5, 2019, accessed: https: // hbr. org / 2019/12/6-signs-your-corporate-culture-is-a-liability

21. HubSpot Retention Score, accessed: https://www.comparably.com/companies/hubspot/retention

22. Jackie Wiles, *Are You a Hybrid Workforce Champion or a Laggard?*, January 13, 2021, accessed: https://www.gartner.com/smarterwithgartner/ are-you-a-hybrid-workforce-champion-or-a-laggard /

23. *The 2021 State of Remote Work*, report by Buffer, accessed: https://buffer.com/2021-state-of-remote-work

24. Molly Fischer, *What Happens When Work Becomes a Nonstop Chat Room*, "New York," accessed: https://nymag.com/intelligencer/2017/05/what-has-slack-done-to-the-office.html

25. Brian Elliot, *Not all Daily Active Users are created equal: Work is fueled by true engagement*, October 10, 2019, accessed: https://slack.com/intl/en-pl /blog / news/work-is-fueled- by-true-engagement

26. Blake Thorne, *How Distractions At Work Take Up More Time Than You Think*, February 13, 2020, accessed: http://blog.idonethis.com/distractions-at- work /

27. *Embracing asynchronous communication*, via GitLab, accessed: https://about.gitlab.com/company/culture/all-remote/asynchronous/

28. Liis Milk, *What It Takes to Become Remote-Ready*, via Scoro, accessed: https://www.scoro.com/blog/becoming-remote-ready/

29. *GitLab Handbook*, via GitLab, accessed: https://about.gitlab.com/handbook/

30. *The Mere Presence of Your Smartphone Reduces Brain Power, Study Shows,* "UT News," June 26, 2017, accessed: https://news.utexas.edu/2017/06/26/the-mere-presence-of-your-smartphone-reduces-brain-power/

31. Jory MacKay, *The Myth of Multitasking: The ultimate guide to getting more done by doing less,* January 17, 2019, accessed: https://blog.rescuetime.com/multitasking/

32. *Social media affecting workplace productivity: Report*, "Business Today", October 18, 2016, accessed: https://www.businesstoday.in/current/

33. Adriana Dahik, etal. *What 12,000 Employees Have to Say About the Future of Remote Work*, "Boston Consulting Group," August 11, 2020, accessed: https://www.bcg.com/publications/2020/valuable-productivity-gains-covid-19

34. *Going remote : Leading dispersed teams*, "The Institute of Leadership and Management," accessed: https://www.institutelm.com/resourceLibrary/going-remote-leading-dispersed-teams.html

35. Matt Torman, *Forbes Insights: A Video-First Culture is Critical for Overcoming the Workplace Challenges of the Future*, "Zoom Blog," February 5, 2020, accessed: https://blog.zoom.us/forbes-insights-video-first-culture-overcoming-workplace-challenges-of-the-future/

36. Jim Dallke, *Meet Spot, an audio tool designed for walking meetings—and the antidote for Zoom fatigue*, March 17, 2021, accessed: https://www.bizjournals.com/chicago/inno/stories/profiles/2021/03/17/spot-audio-walking-meetings.html

37. Geoffrey James, *You Simply Won't Believe How Much Time You Waste in Meetings at Work*, According to MIT, "Inc.", September 23, 2019, accessed: https://www.inc.com/geoffrey-james/you-simply-wont-believe-how-much-time-you-waste-in-meetings-at-work-according-to-mit.html

38. Taylor Locke, *Productivity tips from Elon Musk, Jeff Bezos and Steve Jobs*, "CNBC," September 11, 2019, accessed: https://www.cnbc.com/2019/09/11/productivity-tips-from-elon-musk-jeff-bezos-steve-jobs-and-more.html

39. Ruth Umoh, *Why Jeff Bezos makes Amazon execs read 6-page memos at the start of each meeting*, "CNBC," April 23, 2018, accessed: https://www.cnbc.com/2018/04/23/what-jeff-bezos-learned-from-requiring-6-page-memos-at-amazon.html

40. *Forum on Leadership: A Conversation with Jeff Bezos*, speech video, April 21, 2018, accessed: https://www.youtube.com/watch?v=xu6vFIKAUxk

41. Randall J. Beck, Jim Harter, *Why Great Managers Are So Rare*, accessed: https://www.gallup.com/workplace/231593/why-great-managers-rare

42. Ibid

43. Kathryn Dill, Y*our Next Boss: More Harmony, Less Authority*, "The Wall Street Journal", January 12, 2021, accessed: https://www.wsj.com/articles/your-next-boss-may-be-more-of-a-coach-than-a-dictator-11610467280

44. Joanna Stern et al. *Tech That Will Change Your Life in 2021*, "The Wall Street Journal," Jan 1, 2021, accessed: https://www.wsj.com/articles/tech-that-will-change-your-life-in-2021-11609519215

45. *It's not a meetup*, March 5, 2013, accessed: https://signalvnoise.com/ posts / 3457-its-not-a-meetup

46. Erin 'Folletto' Casali, *Distributed Companies: the Importance of Meeting Face-to-Face*, December 7, 2015, accessed: https://intenseminimalism.com/ 2015 / distributed-companies-the-importance-of-meeting-face- to-face /

47. Stephanie Lee, *Step-by-Step: How We Planned A Retreat For a Remote Team of 75*, May 2, 2017, accessed: https://buffer.com/resources/plan- remote-retreat /

48. *2020 State of Workplace Empathy*, report via Businessolver, accessed: https://www.businessolver.com/workplace-empathy-executive-summary

49. *Radical Candor — The Surprising Secret to Being a Good Boss*, accessed: https://review.firstround.com/radical-candor-the-surprising-secret-to-being-a-good-boss

50. M. Jayanthi, KVR. Rajandran, *A Study on Multicultural Team and the Culture Diversity in Multi-National Companies*, March 2014, accessed: https://www.researchgate.net/publication/270631959_A_Study_on_ Multicultural_Team_ and_the_Culture_Diversity_in_Multi-National_ Companies

51. *Project Management Audit For Remote Teams: A Step-by-Step Guide*, via Remote-how, November 2020, accessed: https://remote-how.com/blog/project-management-audit-for-remote-teams-a-step-by-step-guide

52. *State of Remote Work 2019*, via OwlLabs, accessed: https://resources.owllabs. com/state-of-remote-work/2019

53. Ibid

54. *The 2021 State of Remote Work*, report by Buffer, accessed: https://buffer. com/2021-state-of-remote-work

55. Justin Black, *How Employees Are Feeling: Burnout Rises to Top of Stressor List*, LinkedIn, May 8, 2020, accessed: https://www.linkedin.com/pulse/how-employees-feeling-burnout-rises-top-stressor-list-justin-black/

56. *Working anytime, anywhere: The effects on the world of work, International Labor Organization*, February 15, 2017, accessed: https://www.ilo.org/global/publications/books/WCMS_544138/lang--en/index.htm

57. *Vacation Time Recharges US Workers, but Positive Effects Vanish Within Days*, New Survey Finds, June 27, 2018, accessed: https://www.apa.org/news/press/releases/2018/06/vacation-recharges-workers

58. Sabine Sonnentag, *Psychological Detachment From Work During Leisure Time: The Benefits of Mentally Disengaging From Work*, "Current Directions in Psychological Science," 2012, accessed: https://www.researchgate.net/profile/Sabine_Sonnentag/publication/228079939_Psychological_Detachment_From_Work_During_Leisure_Time_The_Benefits_of_Mentally_Disengaging_From_Work/links/553d073d0cf245bdd7699a41/Psychological-Detachment-From-Work-During-Leisure-Time-The-Benefits-of-Mentally-Disengaging-From-Work.pdf

59. *Why Wordpress.com's Parent Doubled Down on Remote Work, as Giants Like IBM Call Employees Back*, "Inc." accessed: https://www.inc.com/kaitlyn-wang/automattic-wordpress-remote-work.html

60. Taylor Locke, *Productivity tips from Elon Musk, Jeff Bezos and Steve Jobs*, "CNBC," September 11, 2019, accessed: https://www.cnbc.com/2019/09/11/productivity-tips-from-elon-musk-jeff-bezos-steve-jobs-and-more.html

61. David Benjamin and David Komlos, *A Futurist On Uncertainty, Remote Work Burnout, And The Opportunity To Fix Healthcare*, "Forbes," accessed: https://www.forbes.com/sites/benjaminkomlos/2020/06/11/a-futurist-on-uncertainty-remote-work-burnout-and-the-opportunity-to-fix-healthcare/?sh=5ae8c8f6123a

62. Bill Chapell, *4-Day Workweek Boosted Workers 'Productivity By 40%*, Microsoft Japan Says, "NPR," November 4, 2019, accessed: https://www.npr.

org/2019/11/04/776163853/microsoft-japan-says-4-day-workweek-boosted-workers-productivity-by-40

63. Thomas Heath, *A six-hour workday could make you happier, healthier and more productive*, "The Washington Post", April 21, 2017, accessed: https://www.washingtonpost.com/business/economy/will-a-six -hour- workday-help-you-live-longer/2017/04/21/5569f0dc-237b-11e7-b503-9d616bd5a305_story.html

64. Courtney Seiter, *Buffer Is Moving to a 4-Day Workweek for the Rest of 2020*, June 17, 2020, accessed: https://buffer.com/resources/4-day-workweek-2020/

65. *Nguyen Cuy, Vietnam among economies most impacted by climate change: report*, "VN Express," January 28, 2021, accessed: https://e.vnexpress.net/news/news/vietnam-among-economies-most-impacted-by-climate-change-report-4226779.html

66. Corinne Le Quéré et al., *Temporary reduction in daily global CO2 emissions during the COVID-19 forced confinement*, "Nature", May 19 2020, accessed: https://www.nature.com/articles/s41558-020-0797 -x

67. Hannah Ritchie, *Sector by sector: where do global greenhouse gas emissions come from?*, September 18, 2020, accessed: https://ourworldindata.org/ghg-emissions-by-sector

68. *'Tsunami of data' could consume one fifth of global electricity by 2025*, "The Guardian," December 11, 2017, https://www.theguardian.com/environment/2017/dec/11/tsunami-of-data-could-consume-fifth-global-electricity-by-2025

69. Stuart R. Levine et al., *Diversity Confirmed To Boost Innovation And Financial Results*, "Forbes", January 15, 2020, accessed: https://www.forbes.com/sites/forbesinsights/2020/01/15/diversity-confirmed-to- boost-innovation-and-financial-results/?sh = 53fb54f2c4a6

70. Ibid

71. Ibid

72. *Gender Diversity and Corporate Performance*, July 31, 2012, accessed: https://www.credit-suisse.com/about-us-news/en/articles/media-releases/42035-201207.html

73. Brie Reynolds, *Remote Companies Have More Women Leaders, and These Are Hiring*, November 6, 2017, accessed: https://remote.co/remote- companies-have-more-women-leaders-these-are-hiring /

74. Tommy Beer, *Top 1% Of U.S. Households Hold 15 Times More Wealth Than Bottom 50% Combined*, "Forbes", October 8, 2020, accessed: https://www.forbes.com/sites/tommybeer/2020/10/08/top-1-of-us-households-hold-15-times-more-wealth-than-bottom-50- combined/?Sh = 5173c7d95179

75. *2020 Edelman Trust Barometer*, January 19, 2020, accessed: https://www.edelman.com/trust/2020-trust-barometer

76. Klaus Schwab, *Kapitaliści mają obowiązki wobec społeczeństwa*, "Krytyka Polityczna", January 1, 2020, accessed: https://krytykapolityczna.pl/swiat/kapitalizm-interesariuszy-klaus-schwab/

Printed in Great Britain
by Amazon